Bridging Technology and Literacy

Bridging Technology and Literacy

Developing Digital Reading and Writing Practices in Grades K–6

Amy Hutchison and Jamie Colwell

ROWMAN & LITTLEFIELD
Lanham • Boulder • New York • London

Executive Editor: Susanne Canavan
Associate Editor: Carlie Wall
Marketing Manager: Karin Cholak
Production Editor: Christopher Basso
Interior Designer: Jason Rock
Cover Designer: Chloe Batch

Published by Rowman & Littlefield
A wholly owned subsidiary of The Rowman & Littlefield Publishing Group, Inc.
4501 Forbes Boulevard, Suite 200, Lanham, Maryland 20706
www.rowman.com

Unit A, Whitacre Mews, 26-34 Stannary Street, London SE11 4AB

Copyright © 2015 by Rowman & Littlefield Publishers, Inc.

British Library Cataloguing in Publication Information Available

Library of Congress Cataloging-in-Publication Data

Hutchison, Amy, 1979-
  Bridging technology and literacy : developing digital reading and writing practices in grades K-6 / Amy Hutchison and Jamie Colwell.
    pages cm
  Includes bibliographical references and index.
  ISBN 978-1-4422-3494-9 (cloth : alk. paper) — ISBN 978-1-4422-3495-6 (pbk. : alk. paper) — ISBN 978-1-4422-3496-3 (electronic) 1. Language arts (Elementary)—Computer-assisted instruction. 2. Computers and literacy. I. Colwell, Jamie, 1981- II. Title.
  LB1576.7.H87 2015
  372.60285—dc23

                                                                              2015016521

∞™ The paper used in this publication meets the minimum requirements of American National Standard for Information Sciences—Permanence of Paper for Printed Library Materials, ANSI/NISO Z39.48-1992.

Printed in the United States of America

+multimodal pg. 126

Contents

Chapter One

Digital Technology in the Literacy Classroom

This is a book about integrating digital technology into literacy instruction. There are several reasons we have chosen to write this book and why we are advocates for the integration of digital technology into K-6 literacy instruction. Our reasoning is explained throughout this chapter, so if you have any doubts about the role or value of digital technology as it relates to literacy, keep reading. In this chapter, we expand on the following ideas regarding why K-6 teachers should incorporate digital technology into their literacy instruction: (1) the use of digital technology is incorporated Into the Common Core State Standards (CCSS); (2) digital technology can support literacy instruction by helping children share ideas, information and experiences through images, colors, and sounds; (3) digital technology changes the literacy practices we engage in daily and these practices should be reflected in school; (4) teachers have the opportunity and responsibility to model high quality uses of digital technologies for students and their families; (5) schools have the opportunity to ensure equitable access to digital technology and the way in which it is used in the classroom; and (6) teachers have the opportunity and responsibility to help children develop an understanding of the norms of appropriate, responsible, and ethical behaviors related to online rights, roles, identity, safety, security, and communication.

EXPLANATION OF TERMS AND IDEAS

Before we begin, we wish to clarify the terms that you will see throughout this book and the view of digital technology that we take. This clarification is important for understanding the ways that we believe teachers should integrate digital technology into literacy instruction.

1

Digital Literacies

Although the term *new literacies* is often used to describe the skills and strategies related to using digital technology for literacy and language arts instruction, there are many different meanings associated with the term new literacies. Most of those views, but not all, are consistent with the information presented in this book. Therefore, we instead use the term *digital literacies* to explain and describe the skills, strategies, and dispositions that students and teachers develop and use when learning literacy skills with digital technology. We use the definition of digital literacies provided in the 2013 International Reading Association (IRA) cross-journal virtual issue on digital literacies:

> Digital literacies are practices related to critically navigating, evaluating and creating texts using a range of digital technologies. Oftentimes, digital literacies draw upon foundational forms of literacy. Digital literacies enable students to communicate effectively in digital media environments, as well as to comprehend the ever-changing digital landscape (IRA, n.d.).

The practices and skills described in this definition are what we wish to help teachers develop with their students through the ideas presented in this book.

Technology Integration

Another term that we wish to clarify is *technology integration*. To integrate means to make something a part of another larger thing. Thus, when digital technologies are integrated into literacy instruction, they become part of the teaching and learning process that leads to the attainment of literacy skills. It is important to recognize that when digital technology is integrated into literacy, the goal is still to help students become literate. The focus is not on the technology, but on the literacy goals. However, technology can be used to help students develop literacy skills for both print and digital environments.

It should also be noted that by integrating digital tools into classroom instruction, several instructional components will need to change. First, the classroom environment will likely be altered when digital technologies are integrated according to the Common Core State Standards. When using digital technology according to the Common Core Standards, students are collaborating, searching for information online, using digital tools to convey their understanding, and creating many types of digital products. This type of instruction likely represents a shift from the instruction that occurs in many classrooms without technology.

Another aspect of instruction that may need to be altered is the role of teachers. When students are using digital technology, the teacher may need to act more as a facilitator and enabler rather than always providing direct instruction. We have heard it stated that the teacher becomes the "guide on the side" rather than the "sage on the stage." When thoughtfully approached, the teacher can use digital technology to better support diverse learning styles and learning preferences.

Students' roles may also need to change. When integrating digital technology, there are increased opportunities for students to make choices about how they receive information and demonstrate learning. Students may not be used to making these choices and may need instruction in choosing methods and tools that support their learning styles and preferences. Additionally, students can take on the role of experts when using technology and can teach their peers about the function, features, and navigation of digital tools. This shift in roles will likely require a reshaping of classroom culture. However, it will be important that both teachers and students are persistent in trying to adjust to the new roles that technology brings.

DIGITAL TECHNOLOGY IN THE COMMON CORE STATE STANDARDS

Although many arguments have been made against the Common Core State Standards, all but five states in the United States have chosen to adopt the standards. One aspect of the standards that is likely a major change for K-6 teachers is the use of digital technology for literacy and language arts instruction. Although there is not a separate strand for technology, technology is integrated throughout the literacy and language arts standards, implying that being literate means being *digitally* literate (Dalton, 2012). Digital technology is explicitly mentioned in the anchor standards and in many of the individual grade level standards. Additionally, there are many grade level standards in which the use of digital technology is implicit or that require instruction that digital technology could be used to support. The Common Core State Standards Initiative website provides descriptions that offer a portrait of students who meet the CCSS. In regards to the use of digital technology, the site provides the following description:

> They [students] use technology and digital media strategically and capably. Students employ technology thoughtfully to enhance their reading, writing, speaking, listening, and language use. They tailor their searches online to acquire useful information efficiently, and they integrate what they learn using technology with what they learn offline. They are familiar with the strengths and limitations of various technological tools and mediums and can select and use

those best suited to their communication goals (Common Core State Standards Initiative, 2010, n.p.).

To help students work toward these goals, the use of digital technology is explicitly mentioned or implied in the following English Language Arts Anchor Standards:

- CCSS.ELA-Literacy.CCRA.R.7—Integrate and evaluate content presented in diverse media and formats, including visually and quantitatively, as well as in words.
- CCSS.ELA-Literacy.CCRA.W.6—Use technology, including the Internet, to produce and publish writing and to interact and collaborate with others
- CCSS.ELA-Literacy.CCRA.W.8—Gather relevant information from multiple print and digital sources, assess the credibility and accuracy of each source, and integrate the information while avoiding plagiarism.
- CCSS.ELA-Literacy.CCRA.SL.2—Integrate and evaluate information presented in diverse media and formats, including visually, quantitatively, and orally.
- CCSS.ELA-Literacy.CCRA.SL.5—Make strategic use of digital media and visual displays of data to express information and enhance understanding of presentations.

There is much great news about the way that digital technology is integrated into the standards. First, the good news for teachers who are proponents of digital technology is that they will no longer have to defend their reasoning when they are meaningfully integrating technology into the curriculum. Additionally, the standards suggest using digital tools to engage students and require learners to make complex decisions about how, when, and why to use technology rather than simply using technology for the sake of novelty. Further, because technology use is required, resources such as digital devices and professional development will likely have to be provided. We are also hopeful that teachers will be better prepared by their pre-service teacher programs to integrate digital technology as a result of the standards. Therefore, teachers should feel better-equipped overall to use digital technology in their classrooms as a result of these standards.

DIGITAL TECHNOLOGY STANDARDS FOR INDIVIDUAL GRADE LEVELS

Though we previously listed the English Language Arts Anchor Standards that call for the use of digital technology, we also wish to point out indi-

Table 1.1. Common Core ELA Grade Level Standards That Require the Use of Digital Technology

Grade Level	Standard Involving Technology
K	SL.K.2—Confirm understanding of a text read aloud or information presented orally or through other media by asking and answering questions about key details and requesting clarification if something is not understood.
K	W.K.6—With guidance and support from adults, explore a variety of digital tools to produce and publish writing, including collaboration with peers.
1	RI.1.5—Know and use various text structures (e.g., sequence) and text features (e.g., headings, tables of contents, glossaries, electronic menus, icons) to locate key facts or information in a text.
1	W.1.6—With guidance and support from adults, explore a variety of digital tools to produce and publish writing, including collaboration with peers.
1	SL.1.2—Ask and answer questions about key details in a text read aloud or information presented orally or through other media.
2	RL.2.7—Use information gained from the illustrations and words in a print or digital text to demonstrate understanding of its characters, setting, or plot.
2	RI.2.5—Know and use various text features (e.g., captions, bold print, subheadings, glossaries, indexes, electronic menus, icons) to locate key facts or information in a text efficiently.
2	W.2.6—With guidance and support from adults, explore a variety of digital tools to produce and publish writing, including collaboration with peers.
2	SL.2.2—Recount or describe key ideas or details from a text read aloud or information presented orally or through other media.
2	SL.2.5—Create audio recordings of stories or poems; add drawings or other visual displays to stories or recounts of experiences when appropriate to clarify ideas, thoughts, and feelings.
2	L.2.4, part E—Use glossaries and beginning dictionaries, both print and digital, to determine or clarify the meaning of words and phrases.
3	RI.3.5—Use text features and search tools (e.g., key words, sidebars, hyperlinks) to locate information relevant to a given topic efficiently.
3	W.3.6—With guidance and support from adults, use technology to produce and publish writing (using keyboarding skills) as well as to interact and collaborate with others.
3	W.3.8—Recall information from experiences or gather information from print and digital sources; take brief notes on sources and sort evidence into provided categories.
3	SL.3.2—Determine the main ideas and supporting details of a text read aloud or information presented in diverse media and formats, including visually, quantitatively, and orally.
3	SL.3.5—Create engaging audio recording of stories or poems that demonstrate fluid reading at an understandable pace; add visual displays when appropriate to emphasize or enhance certain facts or details.
3	L.3.4, part D—Use glossaries or beginning dictionaries, both print and digital, to determine or clarify the precise meaning of key words and phrases in all content areas.

(continued)

Table 1.1. (*continued*)

Grade Level	Standard Involving Technology
4	RI.4.7—Interpret information presented visually, orally, or quantitatively (e.g., in charts, graphs, diagrams, time lines, animations, or interactive elements on Web pages) and explain how the information contributes to an understanding of the text in which is appears.
4	W.4.2, part A—Introduce a topic clearly and group related information in paragraphs and sections; include formatting (e.g., headings), illustrations, and multimedia when useful to aiding comprehension.
4	W.4.6—With some guidance and support from adults, use technology, including the Internet, to produce and publish writing as well as to interact and collaborate with others; demonstrate sufficient command of keyboarding skills to type a minimum of one page in a single sitting.
4	W.4.8—Recall relevant information from experiences or gather relevant information from print and digital sources; take notes, paraphrase, and categorize information, and provide a list of sources.
4	SL.4.2—Paraphrase portions of a text read aloud or information presented in diverse media and formats, including visually, quantitatively, and orally.
4	SL.4.3—Identify the reasons and evidence a speaker or media source provides to support particular points.
4	SL.4.5—Add audio recordings and visual displays to presentations when appropriate to enhance the development of main ideas or themes.
4	L.4.4, part C—Consult reference materials (e.g., dictionaries, glossaries, thesauruses), both print and digital, to find the pronunciation and determine or clarify the precise meaning of key words and phrases and to identify alternate word choices in all content areas.
5	RL.5.7—Analyze how visual and multimedia elements contribute to the meaning, tone, or beauty of a text (e.g., graphic novel, multimedia presentation of fiction, folktale, myth, poem).
5	RI.5.7—Draw on information from multiple print or digital sources, demonstrating the ability to locate an answer to a question quickly or to solve a problem efficiently.
5	W.5.2, part A—Introduce a topic clearly, provide a general observation and focus, and group related information logically; include formatting (e.g., headings), illustrations, and multimedia when useful to aiding comprehension.
5	W.5.6—With some guidance and support from adults, use technology, including the Internet, to produce and publish writing as well as to interact and collaborate with others; demonstrate sufficient command of keyboarding skills to type a minimum of two pages in a single sitting.
5	W.5.8—Recall relevant information from experiences or gather relevant information from print and digital sources; summarize or paraphrase information in notes and finished work, and provide a list of sources.
5	SL.5.2—Summarize a written text read aloud or information presented in diverse media and formats, including visually, quantitatively, and orally.

Grade Level	Standard Involving Technology
5	SL.5.3—Summarize the points a speaker or media source makes and explain how each claim is supported by reasons and evidence, and identify and analyze any logical fallacies.
5	SL.5.5—Include multimedia components (e.g., graphics sound) and visual displays in presentations when appropriate to enhance the development of main ideas or themes.
5	L.5.4, part C—Consult reference materials (e.g., dictionaries, glossaries, thesauruses), both print and digital, to find the pronunciation and determine or clarify the precise meaning of key words and phrases and to identify alternate word choices in all content areas.
6	RL.6.7—Compare and contrast the experience of reading a story, drama, or poem to listening to or viewing an audio, video, or live version of the text, including contrasting what they "see" and "hear" when reading the text to what they perceive when they listen or watch.
6	RI.6.7—Integrate information presented in different media or formats (e.g., visually, quantitatively) as well as in words to develop a coherent understanding of a topic or issue.
6	W.6.2.A—Introduce a topic; organize ideas, concepts, and information, using strategies such as definition, classification, comparison/contrast, and cause/effect; include formatting (e.g., headings), graphics (e.g., charts, tables), and multimedia when useful to aiding comprehension.
6	W.6.6—Use technology, including the Internet, to produce and publish writing as well as to interact and collaborate with others; demonstrate sufficient command of keyboarding skills to type a minimum of three pages in a single sitting.
6	W.6.8—Gather relevant information from multiple print and digital sources; assess the credibility of each source; and quote or paraphrase the data and conclusions of others while avoiding plagiarism and providing basic bibliographic information for sources.
6	SL.6.2—Interpret information presented in diverse media and formats (e.g., visually, quantitatively, orally) and explain how it contributes to a topic, text, or issue under study.
6	SL.6.5—Include multimedia components (e.g., graphics, images, music, sound) and visual displays in presentations to clarify information.

vidual grade level standards that involve the use of digital technology. Table 1.1 lists the specific K-6 grade level standards that require the use of digital technology.

These standards outline digital literacy skills that students should practice in each grade level. To highlight these skills, we provide an overview of the skills with examples of how they might be targeted in each grade level in Table 1.2.

Table 1.2.   Examples of Teaching CCSS Digital Literacy Skills by Grade Level

Grade Level	Targeted Digital Literacy Skills and Objectives	Example
Kindergarten	• Questioning skills regarding media (e.g., asking and answering questions about key details and requesting clarification)	Students could watch a video or view a website selected by the teacher and orally ask the teacher questions related to content.
1st Grade	• Digital writing skills using electronic tools. • Questioning skills regarding media (e.g., asking and answering questions about key details of information presented through media) • Digital location and search skills using electronic menus.	Students could use Kindles to search for and locate identifying words and ideas about a text selected by the teacher.
2nd Grade	• Digital writing skills using electronic tools. • Comprehension skills to demonstrate understanding of characters, setting, and plot. • Digital location and search skills using electronic menus. • Summary and description skills regarding information presented through media.	Students could practice, with a partner, oral retellings of stories they read or viewed on tablets.
3rd Grade	• Search skills using keywords, sidebars, and hyperlinks to locate information efficiently. • Digital writing skills, including publication and keyboarding. • Locating and summarizing skills related to using digital information. • Comprehension skills regarding information presented in diverse media.	Students could read and respond to a text on a secure education blog site. Then, students could respond to one another's posts on the blog.
4th Grade	• Interpretation skills related to using digital modes of information, such as websites. • Digital writing and publication skills. • Keyboarding skills (e.g., typing one page of information) • Digital search and location skills. • Summary skills using text presented in diverse media.	Students could navigate digital sources to gather information and type a one-page summary of the information they gathered to post to a class blog.

Grade	Skills	Example
5th Grade	• Analysis skills relative to critique of digital texts of literature. • Digital search and location skills. • Comprehension skills related to using multiple digital sources of information. • Digital writing skills, including publication skills. • Keyboarding skills (e.g., typing two pages of information) • Summarization skills relative to comprehending media. • Skills related to creating or locating audio and digital images to create multimodal presentations.	Students could write a digital text with audio and graphics to support their main ideas about a topic.
6th Grade	• Compare and contrast skills relative to critiquing print-based and audio or video experiences of literature. • Skills related to integrating information presented in different media to develop a coherent understanding of a topic. • Digital writing and publication skills. • Keyboarding skills (e.g., typing a minimum of three pages in a single sitting) • Searching and locating skills on the Internet. • Analysis skills regarding credibility of digital sources. • Summary and sourcing skills relative to digital sources (e.g., avoiding plagiarism and providing basic bibliographic information) • Interpretation skills regarding information presented in diverse media and explain how it contributes to a topic, text, or issue under study. • Skills related to incorporating digital technology to clarify presentations (e.g., finding, uploading, inserting graphics or audio)	Students could create a digital slideshow with hyperlinks, written text, and audio to present their understanding about a content area topic.

ENGLISH LANGUAGE PROFICIENCY STANDARDS

Additional standards that guide many schools are the English Language Proficiency (ELP) Standards. The ELP standards align with the CCSS by focusing on the language needed to access the College and Career Readiness Anchor Standards that are part of the CCSS. The ELP standards are not singularly focused on helping ELLs develop language proficiency, but rather, on helping them develop contextualized language proficiency for communicating in ways called for in school settings and for achieving academic success within specific disciplines. Accordingly, the ELP standards are organized into ten broad standards, with grade level standards providing additional specificity and levels of proficiency. Table 1.3 lists the ten standards. The ELP Standards can be used separately or in combination. The standards do not specify curricular or teaching approaches, but rather serve as a guide for understanding what to teach rather than how to teach it.

Although these standards were developed as indicators of language proficiency for English Language Learners, and not as technology-related standards, they necessarily involve the integration of digital technology. The standards make it clear that students must not only have strong receptive language skills, but must also be able to produce oral and written language

Table 1.3.   English Language Proficiency Standards

Standard Number	Standard
1	Construct meaning from oral presentations and literary and informational text through grade-appropriate listening, reading, and viewing.
2	Participate in grade-appropriate oral and written exchanges of information, ideas, and analyses, responding to peer, audience, or reader comments and questions.
3	Speak and write about grade-appropriate complex literary and informational texts and topics.
4	Construct grade-appropriate oral and written claims and support them with reasoning and evidence.
5	Conduct research and evaluate and communicate findings to answer questions or solve problems.
6	Analyze and critique the arguments of others orally and in writing.
7	Adapt language choices to purpose, task, and audience when speaking and writing.
8	Determine the meaning of words and phrases in oral presentations and literary and informational text.
9	Create clear and coherent grade-appropriate speech and text.
10	Make accurate use of standard English to communicate in grade-appropriate speech and writing.

for varying tasks, audiences, and purposes. Students must also be able to interact with each other through oral and written language. For example Standard 2 (as shown in Table 1.3) states that students should "participate in grade-appropriate oral and written exchanges of information, ideas, and analyses, responding to peer, audience, or reader comments and questions." In a digital society, both the consumption and production of language necessarily involves the use of digital technology. In regards to their receptive language skills, students not only need to make meaning from oral face-to-face presentations, but also from multimedia presentations such as videos, podcasts, and slideshow presentations. In terms of producing language, students must be able to speak and write in a variety of ways. In a technology-rich classroom, this language production could include composing blog posts, podcasts, videos, and websites. It could also mean interacting through social media, such as Twitter, or responding to a peer's digital composition. Whatever the task, the use of digital technology often requires that students combine the receptive, productive, and interactive modalities of language in a variety of ways to create meaning through multiple modalities. Accordingly, these standards should be taken into account along with the Common Core State Standards when working with English Language Learners in the classroom. Thus, these standards are included in the sample lesson plans that appear throughout this book.

TECHNOLOGY CAN SUPPORT THE DEVELOPMENT OF TRADITIONAL LITERACY SKILLS

In addition to the ways that technology should be used to develop digital literacy skills according to the standards, technology can also support the development of traditional literacy skills. Numerous classroom studies have illustrated this point. For example, Andes and Clagett (2011) reported on using a class Wiki page, in conjunction with other digital resources, as a space to share writing projects. Students used the wiki page for: (1) fictional story writing; (2) an activity called My Town, where students described and posted links of local places of interest to e-pals in South Africa; (3) poetry writing using Blabberize (www.blabberize.com) to read aloud, record, and post their poems to the wiki with the use of an avatar; (4) biographical writing of someone they admired, which were then recorded with a digital video recorder and placed on the wiki; (5) PowerPoint presentation development through illustration using Pixie 2, a drawing program, and a writing about their families; (6) writing research reports about animals, which they published using Photo Story with links posted to the wiki; and (7) documentation of virtual field trip experiences. It is easy to see how many reading and writing skills could be supported through these digital activities.

Relatedly, Vasinda and McLeod (2011) had students digitally record themselves each week reading a readers theatre script and then uploaded the script to a podcasting or blogging site. Producing the podcasts created an opportunity for students to self-evaluate their reading fluency, and revise and improve their work. The researchers also found that the use of podcasts led to increased reading achievement, as evidenced by higher comprehension scores for students who participated in the readers' theatre podcasting project.

Hutchison, Beschorner, and Schmidt-Crawford (2012) integrated iPads into the curriculum to help students learn how to sequence story events, work on visualization and identify the main idea and supporting details within a text, learn how to retell information, and illustrate cause and effect relationships. Using iPads to learn those skills helped students learn both traditional and digital literacy skills simultaneously. Additionally, the iPads also afforded students the opportunity to easily modify their work, use size, shape, and color to influence their meaning, visually represent text meaning, collaborate more easily, and engage in non-linear reading and writing.

These are just a few of the ways that classroom teachers have used digital technology to support traditional literacy development while also providing students with opportunities to learn digital literacy skills. However, there are abundant examples like these. These studies provide evidence that delivering this type of instruction is possible and can be successful. However, it requires careful planning to ensure that the technology aligns with the curricular goals prescribed by the Common Core State Standards. In chapter 2 we will discuss how teachers can plan this type of instruction and insure that classroom instruction aligns with the Standards and contributes meaningfully to their instruction.

DIGITAL TECHNOLOGY CHANGES
WHAT IT MEANS TO BE LITERATE

Digital technology changes the literacy practices in which we participate in our daily lives. Hence, different skills, strategies, and dispositions are needed to engage in these practices. Accordingly, these practices should be reflected in the school curriculum and opportunities to develop these new skills, strategies, and dispositions should be provided.

Although there are many types of technology users, let's consider a typical adolescent user to explore the digital practices that young learners will one day engage in. According to the Pew Internet and American Life Project (Lenhart, 2014) 78 percent of adolescents (ages 12-17) have a cell phone, and of those with a smartphone, half of them are "cell-mostly" Internet users, meaning that they mostly access the Internet on their phones and not anywhere else. Further, 75 percent of adolescents send and receive text messages, and 63 percent say that they do so daily. The typical adolescent sends sixty text messages per day. Eighty-one percent of adolescents use social networking sites, and 23 percent use twitter. Of those who use social networking sites, 94 percent use Facebook. Given these statistics, consider how these adolescents' digital literacy practices differ from their print-based literacy practices. First, we would suggest that with the ubiquity of these digital tools and practices, students engage in more and different literacy practices than ever before. Additionally, students are more likely to have an audience for the work they produce than ever before. Further, students must be much more critical consumers of information than ever before, given their abundant access to information and the disintegration of textual authority that was once revered in printed texts. Lankshear and Knobel (2007) describe how the web allows for expertise and authority to become distributed and collective, rather than located in individuals and institutions as it once was. This shift in authority and expertise means that students must not only be more critical readers, but they must also be able to collaborate with others since knowledge is collective and created by many individuals working together.

Leu, Kinzer, Coiro and Cammack (2004) suggest that, at minimum, students must be able to do the following in order to be successful online readers:

- Apply problem-solving skills
- Identify problems and seek appropriate solutions
- Locate useful information relevant to problems
- Critically evaluate information, sorting out accurate information from inaccurate information, essential information from less-essential information, and biased information from unbiased information
- Synthesize information across multiple sources
- Rapidly and clearly communicate solutions to others.

Further, students must be able to understand the meaning that is carried in images, color, sound, video, and the other non-textual elements that are prevalent in digital spaces (Kress, 2003). According to the theory of multimodality (Kress & van Leeuwen, 2001; Kress, 2003), processing information presented through these different modes is a different function from the linear, sequential reading of print-based texts. In addition to being able to read these multimodal texts, students must also understand how to write them. Students must understand how the inclusion of graphics, photographs, and colors, as well as the layout of the text, influence their meaning.

Because of the many ways that digital technology changes the literacy practices in which we participate, teaching approaches of the past will not adequately equip students for the unimagined literacies of the future. We have to prepare students to be effective navigators, collaborators, digital communicators, problem solvers, critical consumers, and more. There are many reasons that teachers have difficulty teaching with digital technology (Hutchison & Reinking, 2011), but ultimately we must all work together to ensure that our students are being adequately prepared for the environments in which they read and write.

TEACHERS HAVE THE OPPORTUNITY AND RESPONSIBILITY TO MODEL HIGH QUALITY USES OF DIGITAL TECHNOLOGIES FOR STUDENTS AND THEIR FAMILIES

Viewpoints surrounding digital technology and young children are conflicting to say the least. While we agree that idle time spent in front of a television or computer with no high-quality interactive engagement to promote learning may be detrimental to children's cognitive and physical health, we also agree that multiple learning opportunities for children may be afforded by digital technologies (National Association for the Education of Young Children [NAEYC], 2012). We have thus far addressed multiple advantages of incorporating digital technology into young children's learning experiences, and we now speak to the opportunity and responsibility teachers have to model high-quality uses of digital technology for children and their families.

To inspire how teachers may use digital technology in meaningful and educational ways, we considered the International Society for Technology in Education's (ISTE; 2008) Standards for Teachers, which may be accessed here: www.iste.org/docs/pdfs/20-14_ISTE_Standards-T_PDF.pdf. These standards indicate that to use digital technology to promote high-quality instruction, teachers must facilitate and inspire student learning and creativity, develop and design digital age learning experiences and assessments, and model digital age work and learning (ISTE, 2008). Teachers may consider these standards to prepare high-quality instruction that supports interactive and engaging learning in K-6 classrooms. Studies also indicate the positive effects of digital technology when aligned with such standards. For example, Bogard and McMackin (2012) used video tools (i.e., iMovie) to support third graders in producing personal narratives of created stories, which facilitated learning in English Language Arts and offered students creative license in storytelling. Such use of digital technology encouraged students to carefully consider storylines and practice oral language skills, in conjunction with developing digital literacy skills of video production. Additionally, Hansfield, Dean, and Cielocha (2009) considered how a teacher moved response journals to an online blog format, which created opportunities for the modeling of writing and response. Not only could the teacher respond to students' writing more promptly in such an environment, students also became more aware of their writing and honed writing skills as they were more conscientious of writing that their classmates would also read.

Further, we considered how high-quality instruction often engages parents to become active members in their child's learning and the opportunities digital technology presents for parents to connect with learning in the classroom. For example, a teacher may use a collaborative digital tool to promote online writing and interaction with an adult, such as a parent, who can encourage thinking about a topic or help students develop comprehension skills. Gambrell, Hughes, Calvert, Malloy, and Igo (2011) paired third through fifth grade students with adult pen pals who asked the students comprehension questions about books they were reading. This use of a digital tool provided students with the opportunity to refine comprehension, discussion, and writing skills and gave students an added instructional support system in their learning: the adult pen pals. Incorporating parents into an online project, such as Gambrell and colleagues (2011) did, might provide parents with a clearer window into their child's literacy learning and create connections between school and home life. Teachers may also use such practices to model for parents the types of digital experiences that are positive to students learning. We focus on considerations for using technology to connect with parents in Textbox 1.1.

SCHOOLS HAVE THE OPPORTUNITY TO ENSURE EQUITABLE ACCESS TO DIGITAL TECHNOLOGY AND THE WAY IN WHICH IT IS USED IN THE CLASSROOM

Just as teachers have the responsibility to provide students with engaging and interactive learning opportunities with digital tools, we posit that schools offer equitable access to these tools for all students to engage in digital learning and literacy. Despite the growing number of households in the United States that have Internet and computer access, geographical and income-based disparities limit or prohibit home computer and Internet access for roughly one-third of the nation's population (U.S. Department of Commerce, 2011). Children of these households often do not have daily interaction with digital tools, and a digital divide has become present between students with home

---

Textbox 1.1.

Focus On:
Using Technology to Connect with Parents

Challenge: Often, when we think of using technology to connect with our students' parents, we think about using e-mail or a class blog to remind parents of assignments or school functions. Although parents appreciate these reminders and they are important to students' success in the classroom, this type of use does not always engage parents in their child's learning process.

Consider: Digital technology offers many ways to reach parents and engage them in their child's in-school learning beyond homework or event reminders. How can we use technology to create more active parent engagement?

Tips:
1. Learn what types of technology your students' parents have access to. Most (90 percent) American adults own a cell phone, and over half (58 percent) have smart phones (Pew Internet Research Project, 2014). Think about how you might use these tools as you read the remaining chapters in this book.
2. Think about your existing projects or lessons that students would benefit from working with an adult or a parent and how digital technology might support this work.
3. Hold a digital technology informational session during open house or orientation to show and explain to parents the types of technology that will be used during the school year, and discuss options with them for connecting them to their child's learning.
4. Consider how social media might be used to involve parents in students' learning. Check out chapter 9 for more on social media.

Check Out: Edudemic webpage on *5 Ways to Use Technology to Engage with Parents*

Access the source here: www.edudemic.com/technology-engage-with-parents/.

---

or personal Internet and computer access and those without. Students without Internet and computers at home have fewer opportunities to hone their basic digital literacy skills (e.g., keyboard and navigation tool use) and more advanced digital literacy skills (e.g., text and graphic manipulation to represent ideas, searching for and locating information on the Internet). Accordingly, Leu et al. (2014) found that an achievement gap for online reading ability based on income inequality exists. Yet, school settings can provide opportunities for exploring tools such as digital cameras, audio and video recorders, printers, and other technologies to children who otherwise might not have access to these tools (NAEYC, 2012).

In providing these opportunities, teachers must be mindful of the explicit scaffolding that must accompany instructing students with digital tools. Although mini-lessons in using digital tools may be helpful and necessary, particularly in early childhood and early elementary grades, these digital technologies also offer unique opportunities for collaboration. Students who have more experience using digital technology may themselves serve as tutors or teachers to those students who do not have as much experience. Indeed, research supports the advantages of collaboration when using digital tools in instruction with young students (e.g., Andes & Claggett, 2011; Barone & Wright, 2008; Burnett, Dickinson, Myers, & Merchant, 2006).

Additionally, teachers should consider how to integrate technology into multiple in-class activities instead of relying, for example, on homework that utilizes computers and the Internet, to provide students with experience and practice with digital technology. We encourage teachers to consider the types of mobile technology available that may be checked out when developing homework or out-of-class assignments with digital technology, as not all children will have the same access to digital tools at home. Much of the content in this book will support ideas for this development. Teachers may also devise learning stations in their classrooms that incorporate independent use of technologies, such as digital cameras, iPads, and computers, so that students who have less access to technology engage in similar digital experiences as those students who frequently use digital technology. In this way, teachers and schools promote equity among learners through exposure to digital technologies that will be useful to students as they continue through school, in their everyday lives, and in future careers.

DIFFERENCES IN DIGITAL TECHNOLOGY
USE AMONG DIFFERENT AGED STUDENTS

We want to acknowledge that, although this book is aimed at K-6 teachers, there are important differences in how teachers should integrate technology based on the age and developmental level of their students. Some teachers may be concerned that their students are too young to learn with and about technology. Others may believe that their students already know all there is to know when it comes to digital technology. Neither of these positions is accurate.

In regards to young children, the National Association for the Education of Young Children (NAEYC) posits that "Young children need opportunities to develop the early 'technology-handling' skills associated with early digital literacy that are akin to the 'book-handling' skills associated with early literacy development" (NAEYC 2012, p. 4). Similarly, The International Society for Technology in Education ([ISTE]; 2007) recommends that children have basic skills in technology operations and concepts by age five. However, the NAEYC also cautions that passive use of digital technology is not an appropriate replacement for active learning, engagement with other children, and interaction with adults. Therefore, *how* the technology is used with young children is critically important. Teachers can best serve students with technology by carefully planning and implementing thoughtful instruction and reflecting on and evaluating that instruction to guide classroom experiences. For more information on how the NAEYC views technology use for young children, see the joint position statement on technology by the NAEYC and the Fred Roger's Center for Early Learning and Children's Media at www .naeyc.org/files/naeyc/file/positions/PS_technology_WEB2.pdf.

In regards to older students already knowing it all when it comes to digital technology, research illustrates how this idea is untrue. For example, Hutchison and Henry (2010) found that, although the students they surveyed were *frequent* users of technology and could navigate digital tools, they were not effective at reading and comprehending online. As technology is introduced to older students, the teacher's role will likely need to shift, though. That is, teachers will increasingly become facilitators that guide their students into meaningful explorations with technology rather than simply disseminating information to students.

DIGITAL CITIZENSHIP

A final topic that we turn our attention to in this chapter is digital citizenship. The NAEYC says the following of digital citizenship:

> [It] refers to the need for adults to help children develop an emerging understanding of the use, misuse, and abuse of technology and the norms of appropriate, responsible, and ethical behaviors related to online rights, roles, identity, safety, security, and communication. Adults have a responsibility to protect and empower children—to protect them in a way that helps them develop the skills they need to ultimately protect themselves as they grow—and to help children learn to ask questions and think critically about the technologies and media they use. Adults have a responsibility to expose children to, and to model, developmentally appropriate and active uses of digital tools, media, and methods of communication and learning in safe, healthy, acceptable, responsible, and socially positive ways (NAEYC, 2012, p.10).

As use of digital technology has increased in and out of school, professional organizations have increasingly produced statements and literature on digital citizenship. Among the best known of those is Ribble and Bailey's (2007) Nine Elements of Digital Citizenship. They state that teaching about these elements creates a foundation for helping children navigate the issues they face in an increasingly technological world. Their nine elements are as follows:

1. **Digital Access:** *full electronic participation in society.* Technology users need to be aware that not everyone has the same opportunities when it comes to technology. Working toward equal digital rights and supporting electronic access is the starting point of Digital Citizenship. Digital exclusion makes it difficult to grow as a society increasingly using these tools. Helping to provide and expand access to technology should be a goal of all digital citizens. Users need to keep in mind that there are some that may have limited access, so other resources may need to be provided. To become productive citizens, we need to be committed to make sure that no one is denied digital access.

2. **Digital Commerce:** *electronic buying and selling of goods.* Technology users need to understand that a large share of market economy is being done electronically. Legitimate and legal exchanges are occurring, but the buyer or seller needs to be aware of the issues associated with it. The mainstream availability of Internet purchases of toys, clothing, cars, food, etc. has become commonplace to many users. At the same time, an equal amount of goods and services which are in conflict with the laws or morals of some countries are surfacing (which might include activities such as illegal downloading, pornography, and gambling). Users need to learn about how to be effective consumers in a new digital economy.

3. **Digital Communication:** *electronic exchange of information.* One of the significant changes within the digital revolution is a person's ability to communicate with other people. In the 19th century, forms of communication were limited. In the 21st century, communication options have exploded to offer a wide variety of choices (e.g., e-mail, cellular phones, instant messaging). The expanding digital communication options have changed everything because people are able to keep in constant communication with anyone else. Now everyone has the opportunity to communicate and collaborate with anyone from anywhere and anytime. Unfortunately, many users have not been taught how to make appropriate decisions when faced with so many different digital communication options.

4. **Digital Literacy:** *process of teaching and learning about technology and the use of technology.* While schools have made great progress in the area of technology infusion, much remains to be done. A renewed focus must

be made on what technologies must be taught as well as how it should be used. New technologies are finding their way into the work place that are not being used in schools (e.g., videoconferencing, online sharing spaces such as wikis). In addition, workers in many different occupations need immediate information (just-in-time information). This process requires sophisticated searching and processing skills (i.e., information literacy). Learners must be taught how to learn in a digital society. In other words, learners must be taught to learn anything, anytime, anywhere. Business, military, and medicine are excellent examples of how technology is being used differently in the 21st century. As new technologies emerge, learners need to learn how to use that technology quickly and appropriately. Digital Citizenship involves educating people in a new way—these individuals need a high degree of information literacy skills.

5. **Digital Etiquette:** *electronic standards of conduct or procedure.* Technology users often see this area as one of the most pressing problems when dealing with Digital Citizenship. We recognize inappropriate behavior when we see it, but before people use technology they do not learn digital etiquette (i.e., appropriate conduct). Many people feel uncomfortable talking to others about their digital etiquette. Often rules and regulations are created or the technology is simply banned to stop inappropriate use. It is not enough to create rules and policy, we must teach everyone to become responsible digital citizens in this new society.

6. **Digital Law:** *electronic responsibility for actions and deeds.* Digital law deals with the ethics of technology within a society. Unethical use manifests itself in form of theft and/or crime. Ethical use manifests itself in the form of abiding by the laws of society. Users need to understand that stealing or causing damage to other people's work, identity, or property online is a crime. There are certain rules of society that users need to be aware in an ethical society. These laws apply to anyone who works or plays online. Hacking into others' information, downloading illegal music, plagiarizing, creating destructive worms, viruses or creating Trojan Horses, sending spam, or stealing anyone's identify or property is unethical.

7. **Digital Rights & Responsibilities:** *those freedoms extended to everyone in a digital world.* Just as in the American Constitution where there is a Bill of Rights, there is a basic set of rights extended to every digital citizen. Digital citizens have the right to privacy, free speech, etc. Basic digital rights must be addressed, discussed, and understood in the digital world. With these rights also come responsibilities as well. Users must help define how the technology is to be used in an appropriate manner. In a digital society these two areas must work together for everyone to be productive.

8. **Digital Health & Wellness:** *physical and psychological well-being in a digital technology world.* Eye safety, repetitive stress syndrome, and sound ergonomic practices are issues that need to be addressed in a new technological world. Beyond the physical issues are those of the psychological issues that are becoming more prevalent such as Internet addiction. Users need to be taught that there are inherent dangers of technology. Digital Citizenship includes a culture where technology users are taught how to protect themselves through education and training.

9. **Digital Security (self-protection):** *electronic precautions to guarantee safety.* In any society, there are individuals who steal, deface, or disrupt other people. The same is true for the digital community. It is not enough to trust other members in the community for our own safety. In our own homes, we put locks on our doors and fire alarms in our houses to provide some level of protection. The same must be true for the digital security. We need to have virus protection, backups of data, and surge control of our equipment. As responsible citizens, we must protect our information from outside forces that might cause disruption or harm.

Ribble and Bailey believe that these elements provide a good starting point for guiding students in understanding digital citizenship, but also that they are only the beginning. It is important to note that these elements go beyond basic Internet safety and encourage consideration of how digital technology is used, the skills required to use digital technology in the workplace, and even issues of digital equity. These are critical issues that Ribble (2008) suggests should be explicitly taught to students. We agree that these elements of digital citizenship are of utmost importance and should become a regular part of the school curriculum. Depending on a school's setup and resources, the classroom teacher may or may not be the one who introduces these elements of citizenship. However, we believe that all teachers, regardless of role, should reinforce them as they are using digital technology with students.

HOW THIS BOOK IS ORGANIZED

To help you make the best use of this book, we have organized it in several ways.

Some key features that will help make the book of most use to you are as follows:

Vignettes—The chapters relating to specific types of tools (chapters 3–9) each begin with a vignette describing how a teacher might use these tools and some of the considerations for using them. We encourage you to read these vignettes and consider if the classroom situation described is similar to your own. Consider also what you can learn about integrating the tools that are described into your own classroom through the experience of the teacher in each vignette.

Methods of reading and writing and how to teach them—First, chapters are organized around a particular skill or type of reading and writing and how to integrate digital tools to teach it. For example, chapter 3 is about digital reading and illustrates multiple facets of how elementary students read digital texts and how reading digital texts may be similar to and differ from reading traditional texts. Chapter 4 focuses on using images to convey ideas. Chapter 5 focuses on audio tools, and so on.

Digital tools and lesson Plans—Each chapter also provides examples of digital tools that may assist in teaching the digital skills or method of reading and/or writing being presented. Because there are so many useful apps and websites that we could recommend, we only include a small sampling in this book. However, throughout the book, we suggest places to look for further information. We recommend visiting those sites to learn about additional resources that may be helpful.

Additionally, each chapter provides a sample lesson plan focused on the chapter topic. To serve a broad audience, the lesson plan examples are aimed at a variety of grade levels. However, we believe that each lesson plan could be adapted for most grade levels, particularly since they are based on the Common Core State Standards. The Common Core Standards are similar for all grade levels, but build in complexity with each increase in grade level. Therefore, teachers should be able to modify each lesson plan to increase or decrease the complexity for the desired grade level.

Increasing complexity—The chapters in this book are organized to help teachers build the complexity of the digital tasks in which their students participate. For example, chapter 4 focuses on using images and chapter 5 focuses on using digital audio tools. Once students know how to use images and audio, they can integrate them into their writing, which is the focus of chapter 7. Thus, we have organized the chapters in this way to suggest an order in which you might introduce students to digital activities throughout the year. By familiarizing your students with simple ways to use images and audio tools, you can help them build the skills they will need for more complex digital activities, such as creating and sharing videos or Voice Thread presentations (discussed in chapter 8). By gradually building your students' skills throughout the year, you will be able to help them develop a deeper level of expertise with digital tools and be able to involve them in more meaningful, sophisticated, and authentic uses of digital tools.

Long-range Planning—In this book we also suggest that you consider creating a long-range plan for integrating digital technology into your literacy instruction. We believe that by creating a long-range plan, you can ensure that your students are exposed to a variety of digital tools that will help them build strong digital literacy skills. These skills will in turn mean that they are able to participate in more meaningful uses of digital technology. Accordingly, as you use this book, we suggest that you keep a long-range plan in mind. Rather than selecting one tool or lesson plan to try, we suggest that you consider how you can integrate technology across the year to help students build the digital literacy skills that they need to become better readers and writers.

REFERENCES

Andes, L., & Claggett, E. (2011). Wiki Writers: Students and Teachers Making Connections across Communities. *The Reading Teacher, 64*(5), 345–50. doi:10.1598/RT.64.5.5

Barone, D., & Wright, T.E. (2008). Literacy instruction with digital and media technologies. *The Reading Teacher, 62*(4), 292–302. doi:10.1598/RT.62.4.2

Bogard, J. M., & McMackin, M. C. (2012). Combining Traditional and New Literacies in a 21st-Century Writing Workshop. *The Reading Teacher, 65*(5), 313–23. doi:10.1002/TRTR.01048

Burnett, C., Dickinson, P., Myers, J., & Merchant, G. (2006). Digital connections: Transforming literacy in the primary school. *Cambridge Journal of Education, 36*(1), 11–29.

Common Core State Standards Initiative (2010). Common Core State Standards for English language arts and literacy in history/social studies, science, and technical subjects. Washington, DC: National Governors Association Center for Best Practices and the Council of Chief State School Officers.

Dalton, B. (2012). Multimodal composition and the Common Core State Standards. *The Reading Teacher, 66*(4), 333–39.

Gambrell, L. B., Hughes, E. M., Calvert, L., Malloy, J. A., & Igo, B. L. (2011). Authentic reading, writing, and discussion: an exploratory study of a pen pal project. *The Elementary School Journal, 112*(2), 234–58.

Hansfield, L. J., Dean, T. R., & Cielocha, K. M. (2009). Becoming critical consumers and producers of text: Teaching literacy with Web 1.0 and Web 2.0. *The Reading Teacher, 63*(1), 40–50. doi:10.1598/RT.63.1.4

Hutchison, A., Beschorner, B., & Schmidt-Crawford, D. (2012). Exploring the use of the iPad for literacy learning. *Reading Teacher, 66*(1), 15–23.Author. (2011).

Hutchison, A. & Reinking, D. (2011). Teachers' Perceptions of Integrating Information and Communication Technologies into Literacy Instruction: A National Survey in the U.S. *Reading Research Quarterly, 46*(4), 308–29.

International Reading Association. (n.d.). Retrieved January 6, 2014 from http://onlinelibrary.wiley.com/subject/code/000048/homepage/digital_literacies.html.

International Society for Technology in Education. (2007). NETS for Students 2007 Profiles. Washington, DC: Author. www.iste.org/ standards/nets-for-students/nets -for-students-2007-profiles.aspx#PK-2.

International Society for Technology in Education. (2008). *ISTE standards: Teachers*. Author. www.iste.org/docs/pdfs/20-14_ISTE_Standards-T_PDF.pdf.

Kress, G. (2003). *Literacy in the new media age.* London: Rutledge.

Kress, G., & van Leeuwen, T. (2001). *Multimodal discourse: The modes and media of contemporary communication.* London: Arnold.

Lankshear, C., & Knobel, M. (2007). Sampling "the New" in New Literacies. In M. Knobel & C. Lankshear (Eds.), *A New Literacies Sampler* (Vol. 29, pp. 1–24). New York, NY: Peter Lang.

Lenhart, A. (2014). *Teens and technology: Understanding the digital landscape* [Slideshare Presentation]. Retrieved from www.pewinternet.org/2014/02/25/teens -technology-understanding-the-digital-landscape/.

Leu D., Forzani E., Rhoads C., Maykel C., Kennedy C., & Timbrell N. (2014). The new literacies of online research and comprehension: rethinking the reading achievement gap. *Reading Research Quarterly.* doi:10.1002/rrq.85

Leu, D. J., Jr., Kinzer, C. K., Coiro, J., & Cammack, D. W. (2004). Toward a theory of new literacies emerging from the Internet and other information and communication technologies. In R. B. Ruddell, & N. Unrau (Eds.), *Theoretical models and processes of reading* (5th ed., pp. 1570–1613). Newark, DE: International Reading Association.

National Association for the Education of Young Children. (2012). *Technology and Interactive Media as Tools in Early Childhood Programs Serving Children from Birth through Age 8.* Retrieved from: www.naeyc.org/files/naeyc/file/positions/PS_technology_WEB2.pdf.

Pew Research Internet Project. (2014). *Mobile technology fact sheet.* Retrieved from www.pewinternet.org/fact-sheets/mobile-technology-fact-sheet/.

Ribble, M. (2008). Passport to digital citizenship: Journey toward appropriate technology use at school and home. *Learning & Leading With Technology, 36*(4), p.14–17.

Ribble, M. and Bailey, G. (2007). *Digital citizenship in schools.* Washington, DC: International Society for Technology in Education.

U.S. Department of Commerce (2011). Exploring the digital nation: Computer and Internet us at home. Retrieved from: www.esa.doc.gov/sites/default/files/reports/documents/exploringthedigitalnation-computerandinternetuseathome.pdf.

Vasinda, S., & McLeod, J. (2011). Extending readers theatre: A powerful and purposeful match with podcasting. *The Reading Teacher, 64*(7), 486–97. doi:10.1598/RT.64.7.2.

Chapter Two

Planning for Digital Instruction

Teachers can face many barriers when attempting to integrate digital technology into their instruction. Specific to literacy instruction, in a recent national survey of literacy and language arts teachers (Hutchison & Reinking, 2010), a majority of teachers reported that a lack of understanding about how to integrate digital technology and still teach content standards was a barrier to some extent. Further, teachers reported that they did not know how skilled their students were at using digital technology and that they did not believe that their students had the skills they needed for more complex digital projects. Therefore, this chapter is about helping teachers plan instruction that aligns with the Common Core State Standards and that builds complexity in a way that ensures students have the digital skills that they need to participate in digital learning opportunities. To do this, we will first describe various types of integration. We will then discuss how to create a long-range plan for integrating digital technology into your instruction. Finally, we will present a planning cycle for helping teachers plan lessons that optimally integrate digital technology.

LEVELS OF TECHNOLOGY INTEGRATION

There are many ways to integrate digital technology into the classroom that span from the teacher using technology to assist his or her tasks to students using technology for innovative projects and collaboration. The Technology Integration Matrix, which was created by the Florida Center for Instructional Technology (see http://fcit.usf.edu/matrix/matrix.php), illustrates how teachers can use technology to enhance learning for K-12 students. The matrix identifies the following attributes of technology integration that lead to effective learning environments:

- *Active*—The Active attribute makes the distinction between lessons in which students passively receive information and lessons in which students discover, process, and apply their learning. Student engagement is a key component of active learning.
- *Collaborative*—The Collaborative attribute describes the degree to which technology is used to facilitate, enable, or enhance students' opportunities to work with peers and outside experts. The Collaborative attribute considers the use of conventional collaborative technology tools as well as other kinds of technology tools that assist students working with others.
- *Constructive*—The Constructive attribute describes learner-centered instruction that allows students to use technology tools to connect new information to their prior knowledge. This characteristic is concerned with the flexible use of technology to build knowledge in the modality that is most effective for each student.
- *Authentic*—The Authentic attribute involves using technology to link learning activities to the world beyond the instructional setting. This characteristic focuses on the extent to which technology is used to place learning into a meaningful context, increase its relevance to the learner, and tap into students' intrinsic motivation.
- *Goal-Directed*—The Goal-Directed attribute describes the ways in which technology is used to set goals, plan activities, monitor progress, and evaluate results. This characteristic focuses on the extent to which technology facilitates, enables, or supports meaningful reflection and metacognition.

The Technology Integration Matrix also describes the following levels to which technology can be integrated according to each attribute:

- *Entry Level*—At the Entry level, typically the teacher uses technology to deliver curriculum content to students. Entry-level activities may include listening to or watching content delivered through technology or working on activities designed to build fluency with basic facts or skills, such as drill-and-practice exercises. In a lesson that includes technology use at the Entry level, the students may not have direct access to the technology. Decisions about how and when to use technology tools, as well as which tools to use, are made by the teacher.
- *Adoption Level*—At the Adoption level, technology tools are used in conventional ways. The teacher makes decisions about which technology tool to use and when and how to use it. Students' exposure to individual

technology tools may be limited to single types of tasks that involve a procedural understanding.

- *Adaptation Level*—At the Adaptation level, the teacher incorporates technology tools as an integral part of the lesson. While the teacher makes most decisions about technology use, the teacher guides the students in the independent use of technology tools. Students have a greater familiarity with the use of technology tools and have a more conceptual understanding of the tools than students at the Adoption level. They are able to work without direct procedural instruction from the teacher and begin to explore different ways of using the technology tools.
- *Infusion Level*—At the Infusion level, a range of different technology tools are integrated flexibly and seamlessly into teaching and learning. Technology is available in sufficient quantities to meet the needs of all students. Students are able to make informed decisions about when and how to use different tools. The instructional focus is on student learning and not on the technology tools themselves. For this reason, Infusion level work typically occurs after teachers and students have experience with a particular technology tool. The teacher guides students to make decisions about when and how to use technology.
- *Transformation Level*—At the Transformation level, students use technology tools flexibly to achieve specific learning outcomes. The students have a conceptual understanding of the tools coupled with extensive practical knowledge about their use. Students apply that understanding and knowledge, and students may extend the use of technology tools. They are encouraged to use technology tools in unconventional ways and are self-directed in combining the use of various tools. The teacher serves as a guide, mentor, and model in the use of technology. At this level, technology tools are often used to facilitate higher order learning activities that would not otherwise have been possible, or would have been difficult to accomplish without the use of technology.

The attributes described in the Technology Integration Matrix are consistent with research on how digital technology should be integrated into instruction, as well as the portrait of a competent technology user that is presented in the Common Core State Standards and was discussed in Chapter 1. The purpose of the matrix is to help teachers and technology leaders evaluate how technology is being integrated and to also provide models of effective integration. However, as you consider these characteristics, it is important to recognize that every classroom lesson will likely not integrate every characteristic at the highest level. Rather, as you consider these characteristics, you may find that you are at the entry level of integration with some or all of these attributes.

Your goal, then, should be to try to get to the next level. Technology integration is a complex and ongoing process. A teacher may never feel like he or she is optimally integrating each attribute at the transformative level. However, by setting goals and creating long-range plans for integration, teachers can continue to improve their instruction and create a classroom that builds students' digital literacy skills in a structured way.

Consider the attributes of integration we just described: active, collaborative, constructive, authentic, and goal-directed. What does technology integration look like in your classroom or the classroom of others that you work with? Are students actively engaged in using technology as a tool rather than passively receiving information? Are students using technology to collaborate with others? If you still want to know more about each characteristic, you can see the matrix and video examples of instruction at each level of integration at Technology Integration Matrix website: http://fcit.usf.edu/matrix/index.php. Take a minute to view this site and then ponder each of these attributes and the level at which you are applying each attribute in your instruction. Where are you now and where would you like to go next with your digital integration? The next section of this chapter is designed to help you consider how you can integrate these characteristics into your teaching and do so at increasingly sophisticated levels.

LONG-RANGE PLANNING FOR TECHNOLOGY INTEGRATION

At first, long-range planning for integrating technology into your classroom may seem to be a daunting task. The numerous types of technological tools that currently exist, along with the rapid rate in which new technologies emerge, often complicate the selection and use of technology in early or elementary literacy instruction. To help organize this planning process, we invite you to consider four questions to plan for the types of technology and tools you may integrate and how you will integrate them. After considering the following four questions, we provide a fillable matrix that might be used to outline when you will integrate digital tools during the school year.

- What traditional literacy skills do I want to promote?
- What digital and traditional literacy skills and dispositions do my students bring to the classroom?
- What types of activities (e.g., social, reflective) and learning environment do I typically promote in my classroom to improve students' literacy skills and engage them in literacy learning?
- What digital tools might enhance these skills and activities?

[handwritten margin note: 9sk Questions to]

To illustrate how these questions may guide the long-range planning process, we turn to an example of how a fourth-grade teacher, Ms. Sampson, develops a long-range digital literacy plan and how she might use these questions to consider integrating digital tools throughout the year to promote learning.

① What traditional literacy skills do I want to promote?

To begin long-range planning for her fourth-grade language arts curriculum, Ms. Sampson thinks about the overarching digital and traditional literacy objectives she will target. Her objectives align with state and Common Core State Standards. Broadly, she knows that students must be able to read and comprehend multiple types of text (e.g., fiction, informational, digital, non-prose based) independently and proficiently and make evidence-based predictions based on reading. Further, Ms. Sampson wants her students to be able to make connections and develop topics and ideas through writing. Ms. Sampson also wants her students to be able to engage in conversations and collaborate with one another to develop literacy skills. Finally, as fourth grade begins a heavy focus on content, she must prepare to connect language arts to other content areas to address literacy. Knowing that these are the main goals of her curriculum, she then turns to the types of students she will teach.

② What digital and traditional literacy skills and dispositions do my students bring to the classroom?

Ms. Sampson teaches at a large elementary school that draws students from both suburban and urban areas. Thus, she knows she will have a racially, economically, and academically diverse population of students and learners. After studying the third-grade reading test scores for her students, Ms. Sampson knows she must prepare to teach students at different reading levels. Having been a fourth-grade teacher for multiple years, she also considers that this year may be difficult for some of her students who previously excelled at reading since informational texts may be more difficult to comprehend and fourth-grade curricula emphasizes informational texts. Because her school district places a focus on students using computers beginning in kindergarten, Ms. Sampson decides that most of her students should have basic digital literacy skills, such as typing and using the Internet, although she doubts that her students have acceptable Internet research skills, based on information from other teachers and from her review of professional literature. In addition to this knowledge, to better understand her students' skills, she surveys her students at the beginning of the school year to determine their knowledge and experience using various types of technology such as Kindle e-readers, tablets, such as iPads, online discussion boards, such as blogs, and produc-

-take surveys about what technology they know + how the use it

tion tools, such as podcasts and videos. After collecting this information, she learns that almost all of her students have used an e-reader, most have used an iPad either at home or in school, approximately half of her students have some experience with reading or writing on online discussion boards, but almost none have experience using digital production tools. Ms. Sampson decides that over the course of the year, she will integrate digital tools into her instruction that will build upon each other to build digital literacies and provide ample usage and practice time with each of the tools, beginning with e-readers with which students are most familiar.

③ **What types of activities (e.g., social, reflective) and learning environment do I typically promote in my classroom to improve students' literacy skills and engage them in literacy learning?**

make sure you are using tools that do not divert from the teacher you are!.

After thinking about this collective information, Ms. Sampson addresses the types of activities and learning environment she typically promotes in her classroom to engage all students. She believes that students should work collaboratively and that the teacher should play multiple roles such as instructor, facilitator, guide, and also learner. She plans multiple collaborative and social activities where students must work and think together to improve and extend their learning in literacy. Further, Ms. Sampson believes in multiple opportunities for reflection and consequently will provide numerous reflection activities and assignments for her students to practice reflection. To build skills and literacy learning, she also plans individual self-guided learning activities to promote independence.

→ *think about what kind of teacher you are when planning activities*

④ **What digital tools might enhance these skills and activities?**

To address the fourth and final question, Ms. Sampson visits multiple digital tool recommendation websites to consider different types of technologies and how they might be used to promote learning in classrooms (see for example: http://commoncore.org/maps/resources/digital_resources; www.edshelf.com; http://bit.ly/19fVU9a). She decides that, based on online recommendations and literature about promoting literacy in the content areas, along with her knowledge of her students, she wants to first integrate Kindles to promote reading independence, iPads for both independent learning and collaboration, a class blog for collaboration and idea-sharing, and Diigo (www.diigo.com, a social bookmarking site) for resource organization and collaboration. Ms. Sampson decides to focus on video production and podcasting toward the end of the year to promote reflection and social activity and to use these tools in small groups to support students who are less familiar with using technology for creating, producing, and recording.

To organize and plan her semester, Ms. Sampson uses a long-range planning matrix of digital literacy. This matrix is designed to map out the introduction and continued use of digital technology throughout the school year. Note that Ms. Sampson does not plan to integrate digital tools into each content area each month. She instead focuses on digital literacy skills in one content area per month. She also does not specify apps, online platforms or websites as she wants to stay current with technology and plans to choose the most relevant technology available each month. We believe this matrix, or a variation thereof, may be beneficial to educators considering how to incorporate digital technology into their instruction.

→

CREATING YOUR LONG-RANGE PLAN

We encourage you to consider creating your own long-range plan for integrating digital technology into your literacy and language arts instruction. Through this planning, you should be able to establish a method for building students' digital literacy skills so that you can ensure they have the skills they need for creating digital products in the way called for by the Common Core State Standards. Additionally, this type of planning helps ensure that students are exposed to a wide variety of digital tools, skills, and activities. It can also help teachers be more intentional in integrating technology so that technology does not simply get added in when there is extra time or as an occasional activity. Once you have a long-range plan for integrating technology, you can get to the specifics of individual lessons. We will discuss more about how to plan individual lessons in the next section. First, consider our first steps for thinking about how to integrate digital technology (see textbox 2.1).

PLANNING LESSONS THAT
INTEGRATE DIGITAL TECHNOLOGY

Technology use will look different at every grade level and in every classroom. Even if you have had the opportunity to observe teachers using technology or have received professional development in this area, you still may not be sure how to create a lesson that is right for your classroom or the classrooms of those you work with. Accordingly, Hutchison and Woodward (2014) created the Technology Integration Planning Cycle for Literacy and

Table 2.1. Ms. Sampson's Long-Range Planning Matrix

Month	Digital Tool	General Use of Digital Tool	Digital Literacy Skills Addressed
September	Kindle	• Students will use e-readers to complete independent fiction and nonfiction reading • Students will work in partners to compare highlighting and annotations made with Kindle features • Students will use the built-in dictionary to look up unfamiliar words while reading	• Digital text navigation • Interpreting digital text • Manipulating a digital tool for vocabulary knowledge
October	Kindle iPad	• Students will use note making features of the Kindle to compare characters' actions throughout a work of fiction • Students will use annotation features in apps, such as Evernote, on iPads to make annotations to fiction and nonfiction texts; these annotations will be shared with the class • Students will learn to interpret and create digital images as a way of responding to text	• Digital text navigation • Interpreting digital text • Organizing digital information • Creating and interpreting digital images
November	Kindle iPad blog	• Students will use the Kindle to read an informational text • Students will use iPad apps to create story maps to develop their own stories with similar themes to those as they read on the Kindle • Students will use Evernote to build understanding of nonfiction, informational texts by annotating texts with voice notes and images. • Teacher will develop a class blog for students to respond to prompts about fiction and nonfiction texts.	• Digital text navigation • Interpreting digital text • Organizing digital information • Posting on an online platform

Month	Tools	Activities	Online Skills
December	iPad blog	• Students will continue to develop and write stories using iPad storyboard apps • Students will use iPad apps to write stories and informational texts that include images • Teacher will assist students in posting their completed stories to the class blog for sharing	• Organizing digital information • Navigating an online platform (i.e., blog) • Posting on an online platform
January	iPad Internet blog Diigo	• Teacher will model searching for information on the Google+ community developed for students that contains appropriate websites related to physical science • Students will use iPads apps to access Google+ and read teacher-approved websites • Students will use Diigo either on the iPad or a computer to share and annotate found resources and information • Students will write reflections on the class blog about finding information on the Internet	• Internet research (e.g., searching, navigating, locating information) • Organizing digital information • Navigating an online platform (i.e., blog) • Posting on an online platform • Responding to prompts using an online platform
February	iPad Internet blog Diigo	• Students will use iPad sketch apps to create and annotate timelines in history • Students will view historical photographs and videos on the class blog and reflect on those texts in writing on the blog using prompts and literacy strategies learned in class • In small groups, students will search for and locate information on civil rights leaders on the class Google+ site that they will post to Diigo to annotate and share with the class • Students will learn to use digital graphic organizers to organize the information they collect	• Organizing digital information • Navigating an online platform • Internet research • Posting information on an online platform

(continued)

Table 2.1. (continued)

Month	Digital Tool	General Use of Digital Tool	Digital Literacy Skills Addressed
March	iPad Internet Diigo podcast	• Students will conduct research on the class Google+ site and use print sources to develop written and oral biographies of a U.S. president • Students will use an organizational iPad app to outline their biographies • With teacher guidance and supervision, students will post to Diigo useful Internet resources and annotate those sources with descriptions to share with the class • Teacher will introduce podcasting and model a podcast for students to consider as they begin to develop their oral biographies • Students will learn how to post their podcasts to social networking sites and use social networks to gain further information on their topic.	• Internet research • Organizing digital information • Creating and publishing audio texts using digital technology • Social networking
April	iPad blog podcast video	• Students will use their outlines developed with an organizational iPad app to type their biographies in a Word document • With a partner, students will create a podcast to orally present their biographies to share with the class and a larger audience • With teacher supervision and guidance, students will link their podcasts to the class blog • Teacher will introduce video project and model, with lessons, different components of producing a video	• Creating and publishing audio texts using digital technology • Organizing digital information • Using video-production skills (e.g., filming, script-writing, editing) to create a digital product

May	iPad Internet video	• In small groups, students will begin to develop a video using an iPad about different topics of saving the environment for the school and community • Teacher will assign small groups of students to develop an iMovie about each topic • Each group member will take on a specific role (producer, script-writer, camera person, etc.) • Students will create outlines for the movies using an organizational iPad app • Students may use approved Internet sites and texts to develop ideas for their movie • Students will film, organize information, and develop movies using iPad apps (e.g., Evernote, iMovie)	• Organizing digital information • Video-production skills (e.g., filming, script-writing, editing) to create a digital product
June	iPad blog video	• Students will make final edits and post completed movies to the class blog	• Video-production skills (e.g., filming, script-writing, editing) to create a digital product • Publishing video texts on an online platform

Textbox 2.1.

Focus On:
First Steps

Challenge: It is sometimes daunting to integrate digital technology for the first time or different types of digital technology into an already full curricula. There is also a learning curve that comes with incorporating digital technology into lesson plans and instruction.

Consider: Just as we have to learn to use different methods and activities in our instruction to best engage students in learning, we should also learn about new types of digital technology to support students' learning in a global, technology-driven society. However, we don't have to learn everything in a day!

Tips:
1. Take baby steps. You may feel comfortable selecting five new types of digital technology to use in your lessons per year, or you may only want to tackle two for the year. As long as you're using digital technology to support student learning, you're on the right track!
2. Think about ways that you can enhance current projects or lessons with digital technology so as to not reinvent your lessons.
3. Survey your students about their digital skills. What do they already know how to do with digital technology, and how can you use these skills to create readily useable lessons?
4. What types of digital technology does your school/district offer? Start with resources that are readily available and perhaps consider writing a grant or seeking donations for technology that you would love to try but do not have access to.
5. We love group or partner work with digital technology! Let students help one another as they create and learn with digital technology.

Check Out: *Technology Integration Planning Cycle for Literacy and Language Arts* (see p. 37)

Read on as we discuss a planning cycle to help you think about and plan for digital technology in your literacy and language arts lessons.

Language Arts (TIPCLLA) to assist teachers in planning instruction into which digital technology is integrated.

As can be seen in Figure 2.1, the TIPCLLA involves seven guiding elements. The first element is ***identifying the instructional goal***. Rather than being guided by the technology, every lesson should begin and end with the instructional goal, which is determined by a teacher's state standards, long range plans, and daily learning goals. In most cases, it is critical that the

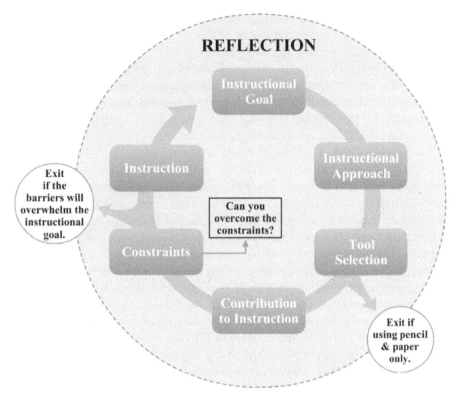

Figure 2.1.   The Technology Integration Planning Cycle for Literacy and Language Arts.

teacher identifies the learning goal before identifying how the technology will be used. Otherwise, the instruction may become only about the technology, rather than helping students meet literacy and language arts standards. Likewise, it is important to end a lesson by reflecting on the lesson and determining if the lesson adhered to the instructional goal. This reflection is particularly important with lessons involving digital technology since it is easy to let the focus be on the technology when problems arise, when students have difficulty with the technology, or when the technology has lots of bells and whistles that would be interesting to explore, but are not necessarily useful or instructional.

Upon identifying the instructional goal, the teacher should then determine an appropriate *instructional approach*. According to Hutchison and Woodward (2014), teachers can do this by determining the extent to which the learning should: (a) be teacher or student centered; (b) be convergent or divergent (should students develop similar understandings or draw their own conclusions?); (c) involve relevant prior experiences with the topic and with the technology that will be used; (d) facilitate a more surface-level or deep understanding of the topic. This decision may vary by the phase of instruction and within a lesson; (e) be longer or shorter in duration; (f) involve more or less structured learning; (g) take place in a whole group, small group, or individual configuration; and (h) involve additional resources.

Next, the teacher should *identify the digital tool(s)* that will help address the instructional goal using the instructional approach that was determined most useful for instruction. This part of the process may initially be based on the digital devices that are available to the teacher. For example, if a teacher has a class set of iPads available but no other devices, then he or she must use iPads. However, there are many ways that iPads can be used, so many decisions must still be made. For example, would the instructional goal be best assisted by using the iPads to search for information online, by using a specialized app, or by using the built-in camera? If an app would best suit the instructional goal and approach, then the type of app must be selected. Determining what technology to use and how to use it can be a difficult part of the process, but is made easier when the pre-determined instructional goal and approach are guiding the process. For example, if a teacher knows that she wants students to work in small groups to publish a well-informed opinion statement on a controversial issue, then the teacher may be able to narrow the options down to using the Internet to find the needed information, using a graphic organizer app for developing and organizing ideas, or using a podcasting app for creating and publishing a recording of their opinion statement. From this point, the teacher will still need to determine the specific apps that will be used, but has narrowed the selection process by first determining the app types. There are many useful websites that provide app descriptions and reviews to help find appropriate apps once you know what type of app you are looking for. We recommend visiting http://bit.ly/1kRXSrf, which provides a long list of app recommendation sites and podcasts. If, upon searching for a digital tool to meet your needs, you are unable to find the right tool, you may consider not using a digital tool at all. Although it is important to integrate digital tools into instruction, it is also important to be sure that the tools help meet the instructional goal rather than distracting from it. If you cannot find a tool appropriate for your instructional goal, then we recommend asking an instructional leader or fellow teacher for help. If you are still unable to find the right tool, then we recommend that you learn more and explore different options before integrating technology.

Following your successful tool selection, it is time to consider the *contribution that the technology will make to the instruction*. This part of the process involves determining if you are maximizing your instruction by helping students to learn both traditional and digital literacy skills with the instruction you have planned. Ask yourself if the lesson addresses both digital and non-digital standards. For example, you could design a fifth grade lesson in which you had students read an informational text and determine the main ideas. You could then ask them to explain why those ideas are important and supported by key details through the use of a presentation app. Through an app such as Explain Everything, they could include images to support their ideas and then also orally explain their thinking. In this case, you would be addressing the following digital and non-digital fifth grade Common Core standards:

• CCSS.ELA-Literacy.RI.5.2—Determine two or more main ideas of a text and explain how they are supported by key details; summarize the text.
• CCSS.ELA-Literacy.SL.5.5—Include multimedia components (e.g., graphics, sound) and visual displays in presentations when appropriate to enhance the development of main ideas or themes.

This is a simplistic example, but it illustrates how integrating digital technology helps students learn a traditional literacy skill (determining main ideas), but also helps them to learn digital skills such as creating multimodal presentations. In this case, the use of the digital tool is making an important contribution to the instruction because it addresses a digital Common Core standard. Further, by considering all the contributions that the digital tool makes to the instruction before considering the difficulties you may face in implementing it, you can feel assured that your integration efforts are worthwhile.

The next step in the planning process is to consider the possible *constraints of the tool* and the potential difficulties that you may have in implementing the lesson. By considering the possible constraints first, you may be able to come up with solutions or at least be prepared for challenges as they arise. Possible constraints of digital tools that you may use could be something as simple as the fact that the free version of an app you are using does not allow users to save their work. By considering this potential constraint in advance, you could come up with a solution rather than avoiding using the app all together. In this case, the solution could be to have students take a screen shot of their work before closing the app. Other barriers you may face could be related to classroom management issues, physical space in the classroom, students' lack of experience with a particular tool, time management, etc. Again, by thinking through the constraints of the tools themselves and the potential classroom issues in advance, you may be able to come up with solutions that will make the instruction more successful and everyone less frustrated. However, it is also important to consider that the constraints may be too much of an obstacle and the digital tool should not be used in the way planned. If you are unable to come up with solutions, at this point you should go back in the cycle to select a different tool. If you are unable to select an appropriate digital tool, then perhaps digital technology should not be used in the lesson you are planning. At this point, you should exit the planning cycle if you believe that you would be unable to overcome the constraints of using the digital tool. It is important to remember that many digital tools may present challenges and those challenges may only get better by gaining experience with the tools and finding potential solutions. However, that type of problem solving should be balanced with the goals of instruction. If the technological challenges overwhelm the instructional goal, then, in those cases, using digital tools may not be worthwhile.

The final components of the TIPCLLA are *considering instruction and reflection*. At this point, you know what digital tool you are using, how it supports your instructional goal, and have come up with solutions for possible difficulties. Now it is time to consider the aspects of instruction that will need special consideration because you are integrating digital technology. For example, you may realize that students will need special instructions about how to use the app you have selected. Alternately, you may have to consider how students will submit the digital work they create since there will be no paper copy. If you are using mobile devices, you may need to consider where students will be allowed to use the devices. Again, by considering these aspects of instruction in advance, you can help make the instruction more successful. Finally, as the instruction is being implemented and after it is complete, you should reflect on the lesson to determine if you were able to meet your instructional goals or if the technology interfered with that goal. If you were able to successfully meet your goals, you should consider what the successful aspects of the lesson were that made that possible. If the technology overwhelmed the instructional goal, you should consider why that happened and what aspects of the instruction you could change in the future to make the instruction more successful.

Finally, each stage of the TIPCLLA involves asking important questions about the planning and implementation of instruction. Accordingly, Table 2.2 provides a list of questions that teachers should ask at each phase of instructional planning with the TIPCLLA.

By using the TIPCLLA to plan your instruction, you will have a process for guaranteeing that you have considered many important elements of instruction and have a plan in place to ensure that you are focused on important instructional goals rather than the technology you are using. We encourage you to keep this planning cycle in mind as you read about the ways of using digital tools that are found in this book. Throughout the chapters, we will be providing example lesson plans that integrate the elements of this planning cycle. Be on the lookout for those components in the lesson examples and consider how you could use the cycle in your own planning.

Table 2.2. Questions to Ask at Each Phase of the Technology Integration Planning Cycle

Planning Phase	Questions to ask
Determining the Instructional Goal	• What standards do I want to address? • What do I want students to know and be able to do?
Determining the Instructional Approach	To what extent should the learning: a. Be teacher or student centered? b. Be convergent or divergent (should students develop similar understandings or draw their own conclusions?) c. Involve relevant prior experiences with the topic? d. What digital skills students will need to learn in order to participate in the lesson? Do they have them? e. Facilitate a more surface-level or deep understanding of the topic? f. Be longer or shorter in duration? g. Involve more or less structured learning? h. Take place in a whole group, small group, or individual configuration? i. Involve additional resources?
Selecting the Digital Tool	• What tool, app, or website will help me achieve my instructional goal using the instructional approach I have selected? • How can I find the resources I need? • Am I still adhering to my instructional goal? (**If no, exit the planning cycle**)
Determining the Contribution to Instruction	• Does this use of technology provide the opportunity to learn both digital and non-digital literacy skills (or content standards and digital literacy skills)? • Does this use of technology require students to engage in the types of multimodal production and/or consumption required by the Common Core standards?
Determining the Potential Constraints	• What are the potential constraints of using this technology for instruction? • Do constraints of using the digital tool overwhelm the instruction? • Can I overcome the constraints? (**If no, exit the planning cycle**)
Instructional Considerations	• How might my instruction need to differ from normal as a result of integrating technology in this way? • What special factors do I need to consider (classroom space, submitting assignments, etc.?)
Reflection	• To what extent did I adhere to my instructional goal? • What helped or hindered your students' abilities to meet the instructional goal?

TAKE ACTION!

1. Use the example long-range technology integration plan provided in this chapter to develop your own long-range plan. Remember that you do not have to strictly adhere to what you write, but having a plan in mind can help you to strategically integrate technology on an ongoing basis.
2. Try planning a lesson with the Technology Integration Planning Cycle for Literacy and Language Arts. Did you have difficulty with any particular part of the planning? Consult with a coach or colleague to develop your expertise in the areas that were difficult for you.

REFERENCES

Hutchison, A., & Reinking, D. (2010). A national survey of barriers to integrating information and communication technologies into literacy instruction. In R. Jimenez, V. Risko, M. Hundley, & D. Rowe (Eds.), *Fifty-Ninth Yearbook of the National Reading Conference* (pp. 230–43). National Reading Conference. Milwaukee, WI.

Hutchison, A., & Reinking, D. (2011). Teachers' Perceptions of Integrating Information and Communication Technologies into Literacy Instruction: A National Survey in the U.S. *Reading Research Quarterly, 46*(4), 308–29.

Hutchison, A., & Woodward, L. (2014). A Planning Cycle for Integrating Technology into Literacy Instruction. *Reading Teacher, 67*(6), 455–64. DOI: 10.1002/trtr.1225.

Chapter Three

Digital Reading in the Classroom

Mrs. Johnson is a teacher at Southview Elementary School. Her principal has just set a new school-wide goal for all teachers to regularly integrate digital technology into their literacy instruction. Mrs. Johnson has access to a cart of iPads that is shared among several grade levels and can be reserved and checked out when available, a computer lab, three desktop computers in her classroom, and a set of five iPads that stay in her classroom. To help the teachers meet the principal's technology integration goal, the literacy coach will be providing professional development to the teachers on how to use the Technology Integration Planning Cycle for Literacy and Language Arts to plan their instruction. The literacy coach is also supporting the teachers in setting up a long-range plan for integrating technology throughout the year. As discussed in chapter 2, the teachers will start with simple uses of digital technology and build the complexity of the students' digital tasks throughout the year. The literacy coach will also be introducing new apps and websites to the teachers each month and providing them with sample lesson plans demonstrating how to integrate the sample tools to teach Common Core English Language Arts Standards. This month, the literacy coach has introduced the teachers to some sites with free digital books and showed them how to use a text annotation tool that will allow students to add notes to the digital books they read. Accordingly, Mrs. Johnson has planned a lesson in which her students will be doing a close reading of a digital text about a science topic and using a text annotation site called Diigo to highlight and make notes about important words and details. Her lesson is presented in Figure 3.2.

DIGITAL READING

When reading moved into the digital age, the term reading took on new meaning and began to carry different implications for student success in reading. Digital reading, or the act of consuming texts on a digital device (i.e., e-reader, tablet) or platform (i.e., blog, wiki, website), utilizes traditional reading skills, such as decoding and fluency, but also often requires students to use other skills, such as navigating texts, listening to audio, or viewing video along with texts. Even the most basic e-reader device (e.g., a Kindle) that simply transfers a book or story to a digital format comes equipped with features such as page and table of contents navigation, a digital dictionary, and highlighting features, creating a different reading experience than a print-based text may offer. Because digital reading encompasses a wider range of skills, some, such as Lankshear and Knobel (2011), refer to these skills as literacy skills, rather than reading skills and often note that these skills are new literacies as they are inherently different than traditional reading. Although we do not place a large focus on the evolving jargon surrounding literacy in the digital age in this book, we want the reader to consider how instruction might be affected by integrating new literacies, such as reading digital texts, and how students grapple with new literacies.

A primary difference between traditional reading and digital reading pertinent to classroom instruction is the distinct difference between the types of texts used. For example, traditional reading typically entails print-based, word-driven text, sometimes accompanied by a 2-D image. Yet, digital reading expands the definition of text, and a first step that teachers should consider when incorporating new technologies into their classroom is the redefinition of text and what sources may be considered to be texts (Booth, 2006). In this chapter, we refer to reading digital texts such as websites, e-reader books and stories, and tablet applications (hereafter referred to as apps) that support stories, poems, books, and nonfiction informational texts. In the chapters that follow, we broaden the range of text and consider texts such as, but not limited to, digital images, podcasts, and videos. This expanded notion of text has changed the way teachers must consider reading in their instruction and how students might respond to such texts.

Because our students live multimodal lives in which they experience and interact with tools (e.g., the Internet, television, iPads) that involve audio, visual, and often interactive features, the classroom shift from traditional reading to digital reading is often engaging and motivating for students as it mimics many aspects of their out-of-school lives. Thus, an important part of reading digital texts includes the response that students have to that text and how teachers have their students respond to digital text. These transactions that students have as they respond to text highlight the importance of reader response (Rosenblatt, 1968) when incorporating digital reading into lessons, and we provide digital tools and examples throughout this chapter to consider various modes of response. By having students respond to the digital texts they read, the teacher may better identify both traditional and new literacies with which students may struggle or excel. Often digital reader response tools allow unique insight into how students comprehend a text, and reading on digital devices and observing or recording students as they do so may offer perspective on the types of aids (e.g., visual, auditory) necessary for student success in reading. For example, Larson (2010) found that when second-grade students were provided Kindles for reading books, they used tools and features such as font-size adjustment, auditory text-to-speech features, highlighting tools, the built-in dictionary, and search features. Students also used annotation or note-making tools to support their reading, which offered teachers insight into students' meaning-making processes.

COMMON CORE CONNECTIONS

The Common Core State Standards (CCSS) also highlight the importance of digital reading to support student learning in language arts. Anchor standard CCSS.ELA-LITERACY.CCRA.R.7 explicitly states that students should be able to "Integrate and evaluate content presented in diverse media and formats, including visually and quantitatively, as well as in words" (CCSS, 2010). However, all of the English Language Arts anchor standards could easily be applied to incorporating digital reading into instruction. For instance, students could use e-readers and tablets to analyze events and ideas as they interact over the course of a text (CCSS.ELA-LITERACY.CCRA.R.3). E-readers might be particularly useful for close reading to determine what the text says explicitly and to make inferences from it since e-readers offer multiple features and functions that allow students to comprehend text and make notes to consider inferences (CCSS.ELA-LITERACY.CCRA.R.1). Tablets also host apps that support textual analysis through note making, graphic organizers, and drawing tools for story mapping that can support students in analyzing the structure of texts (CCSS.ELA-LITERACY.CCRA.R.5), in analyzing and determining central ideas and themes and summarizing supporting details and ideas (CCSS.ELA-LITERACY.CCRA.R.2), and in comparing two or more texts addressing the same themes or topics to compare authors' approaches (CCSS.ELA-LITERACY.CRA.R.9). A bridge is thus created between the CCSS and digital reading that supports a broader definition of reading and expands the types of texts commonly used in K-6 education.

The next section describes several ways that digital texts can be introduced and used in the classroom. It is important for us to note that there is far more to know about helping students read and learn from digital texts, particularly non-linear websites, than can be covered in this chapter. However, this chapter can guide you in getting started and expanding your instruction with digital text in your classroom.

DIGITAL TEXTS IN THE CLASSROOM

We regard this chapter as an introduction to the content included in the remainder of this book. Each chapter following this one will, in some way, address reading or production of digital texts as anything that can be read, viewed, or listened to may be considered a digital text. Here we provide an overview of basic examples of digital reading, such as the use of e-readers, a brief overview of reading websites on the Internet, and annotating digital word-based texts during reading. We also provide sample tools to consider as a more comprehensive list of tools and resources is available in Table 3.1 at the end of the chapter. Each chapter following this one will address increasingly more complex types of digital texts and how to structure students' reading and production of those texts. We ask the reader to consider the following sections as the first step into the world of digital reading. For those of you more comfortable with incorporating digital technology into your K-6 curriculum, use these sections as a refresher. For those who are just beginning their journey into the world of digital technology in instruction, let these sections begin to expand your ideas about how digital reading may play a role in your classroom.

Navigating Digital Texts

Digital texts can appear in many different formats. For example, if you are reading a website, text may appear in paragraphs or only short segments. There may be hyperlinks to view, multiple tabs to view, images to read, and videos to view. Alternately, if you are reading with a storybook app, the text generally appears in the same linear format as a printed text would. However, storybook apps often feature audio support and may have accompanying activities that can be accessed by touching images on the screen or following a link of some kind. If you are reading with a digital reading device such as a Kindle, the text will also mimic printed text, but will have additional features that can be accessed, such as a dictionary feature that can be activated by touching a word on the screen. Further, you can change the font size, add notes, and highlight text with digital readers and digital reading apps. All of these features are intended to support the reader. However, it is important that we teach students how to access and effectively use these tools and read online so that the features support, rather than hinder, them.

Before providing students, particularly younger students who may not have as much digital experience, with e-readers, such as Kindles or iBooks on an iPad, teachers should be prepared to model reading from such tools. Consider using e-readers with color displays during read-alouds. Just as you would pause and ask questions or include explanatory comments during a read aloud with a print book, you can do the same with an e-reader. However, these think-alouds might include how to highlight information of interest or how to enlarge font to better understand a passage. Stopping at important vocabulary words and using the built-in dictionary or text-to-voice features may also be useful for students to learn how to navigate and use support tools with e-readers. Although today's K-6 students are commonly referred to as digital natives, not all students will be familiar with reading from e-readers, and read-alouds using such devices may support their use.

Further, before having upper elementary students begin to read from websites to find information for classroom activities, direction on finding and evaluating reliable sources should become part of instruction. One way of helping students evaluate websites to determine if they will be useful is the WWWDOT framework (Zhang, Duke, & Jiminez, 2011). This framework guides students in asking the following questions about sites they are viewing:

- **W**ho wrote this and what credentials do they have?
- **W**hy was it written?
- **W**hen was it written?
- **D**oes it help meet my needs?
- **O**rganization of the site?
- **T**o-do list for the future (track resources that could be used to enhance learning on the topic).

By teaching students to follow this framework, you can support them in thinking critically in regard to whether the information they access is credible. This framework also assists in their navigation of the text by teaching them an approach to making sense of and organizing a vast amount of information on a site by recording resources that could be used in the future. This part of the framework helps students avoid getting lost in a string of links by encouraging them to completely view and assess the website they are using before linking to other resources.

Annotating Digital Texts

There are many tools that allow the reader to annotate digital texts. One example of this type of tool is GoodReader. GoodReader makes it possible to annotate portable document format files (PDFs) by highlighting, underlining, drawing shapes, and writing and typing notes directly on the text. For teachers, this means that you can have students write directly on text, and each students' text annotations will differ to highlight the manner in which they read and comprehended the text. The text just needs to be in PDF format. See Figure 3.1 for an illustration of annotation with the GoodReader app. Again, these types of tools allow teachers to study and consider how students analyze and read texts and provide a window to students' reading comprehension skills to support detailed and individual assessment.

A similar tool that allows the reader to annotate digital text is Evernote. Evernote permits the user to make written notes, capture photos, create audio and voice notes, and organize them into a single digital notebook that can be shared with others. Tools such as these provide new ways of interacting with texts. In an elementary classroom, these types of apps could be used to guide students in close reading of texts, as prescribed by the Common Core State Standards. We also like the Subtext app (https://web.subtext.com/) to support close reading as teachers can embed notes or discussion prompts in

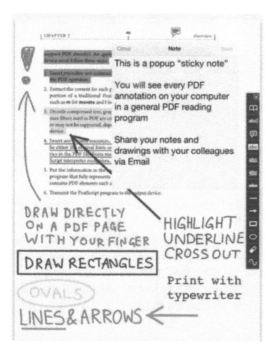

Figure 3.1. Example of Text Annotated with the GoodReader App.

almost any digital text to have students engage more actively during reading. Subtext allows teachers to download books or articles for students to read and annotate within text. Figure 3.2 provides a screenshot of the layout of a book being read in Subtext.

You can also link your Subtext app to social learning platforms, such as Edmodo (www.edmodo.com), and that we will discuss in a subsequent chapter, to easily access class readings or books. An overview of the Subtext app with teacher feedback may be viewed at http://vimeo.com/70265199. With this app students must stop and consider important text features or content while reading and respond to prompts about those features, based on the

Figure 3.2. Screenshot of the layout of a book being read in Subtext

Figure 3.3.   Screenshot of an assignment page in Subtext.

assignment provided by the teacher (see Figure 3.3 for a screenshot of an assignment page).

This type of tool also allows the teacher to track student learning and reading of texts through annotations. Using the digital annotation features of these tools help students draw attention to important aspects of the text by encouraging students to more carefully read and consider the texts.

Another type of annotation for online digital texts is social bookmarking and note-taking. Diigo is a popular app and website (www.diigo.com) that facilitates shared annotation and navigation of websites. It allows the user to annotate and organize text, archive links to webpages, and share links and notes with other users for feedback and discussion. Whereas Evernote may be more useful for individual or partner annotation activities, Diigo involves whole-class sharing of digital texts and resources, with accompanying annotations. The teacher plays an active role when using Diigo because they set up the class network for resource sharing and can model and provide feedback to the bookmarks students have posted. Teachers may also find digital note-taking tools useful for assessment of students' reading skills and use these tools for anecdotal records to conduct formative assessment. The use of digital devices to take and organize student-record notes allows for easy collection and organization of student-focused notes, which promotes instructional decision-making and individualized literacy support for students (Bates, 2013). Read more about annotation in the Focus box below (see textbox 3.1).

Using Audio to Support Digital Reading

Although we focus more directly on audio in chapter 4, we include here that another way that digital texts can support readers is through audio enhancement features. Many popular children's books such as *The Cat in the Hat* (Dr. Suess, 1957), *Pat the Bunny* (Kunhardt, 1962) , and *Green Eggs and Ham* (Dr. Suess, 1960), have tablet apps that read a storybook aloud while highlighting the word being read to show one to one correspondence. These types of apps can be useful for beginning readers, for English Language Learners (ELLs), and for more mature readers that need help becoming motivated or engaged with text. Additionally, there are many websites with videos of stories being read aloud. For example, www.storylineonline.net features a variety of storybooks being read aloud by celebrities. Similarly, Barnes and Noble features online story time on their website. Although multiple interactive storybooks are available as apps, we do encourage teachers to carefully review these texts as the quality of digital books and the features they offer vary. A quick Internet search may provide useful reviews of apps, and multiple tutorial or review videos are available on sites such as YouTube that help educators determine the quality of a storybook app and how to utilize all of the features it offers.

Free Digital Texts

An exciting aspect of digital text is that there are now many free books available online. Teachers can access these books to supplement their classroom materials and provide students with experience navigating digital texts. This

---

Textbox 3.1.

Focus On:
Annotation

Challenge: In elementary grades, when students are learning and honing writing and summary skills, annotation may be difficult for students to master or understand. Some students may find it challenging to write in words what they think a source is about or represents.

Consider: Many age-appropriate digital tools exist that allow students to annotate with text or with images.

Tips:
1. Engage in a think-aloud with students as you read and annotate digital and traditional texts. Let students see the difference between annotating digital and traditional text, paying particular attention to the differences in text structure and focus for annotation (e.g., a digital text may have images, links, and audio features that should be considered in annotation).
2. Treat annotation as you would note-making procedures in instruction. Some students may benefit from a fill-in-the-blank or prompting guide to make notes about a source. Younger elementary students may be encouraged to use image and drawing tools for annotation.
3. If you use an annotation tool, such as Diigo, provide plenty of teacher-generated annotations as a model for students.
4. Have students practice whole-class annotation of sources by having them dictate to you as you type their summaries, so that you may provide feedback.
5. At first, focus predominantly on the content of the annotations, instead of the mechanics of writing, encouraging students to provide their opinions in the annotations to guide other classmates in using sources.

Check Out: *Screen Draw* (https://addons.mozilla.org/en-US/firefox/addon/screen-draw/)

Screen Draw allows students to take a snapshot of any webpage or computer screen and draw or type text over the page to create annotations.

---

experience is necessary and important because many digital books have enhanced features that students should know how to use effectively to become digitally literate. Further, grade level Common Core standards state that students should be able to use digital text features such as hyperlinks. For example, the CCSS indicate that a third grade student should be able to use text features and search tools (e.g., key words, sidebars, hyperlinks) to locate information relevant to a given topic efficiently (CCSS.ELA-LITERACY. RI.3.5). Accessing these free digital texts can provide students with experience reading online that is different than reading websites. One example of a site offering free digital books is www.wegivebooks.org. This site offers free books of many different genres and for a variety of ages. We particularly like that this site offers many informational books, which are often less common in the classroom.

Virtual Bookshelves Based on Topic/Reading Level

Another interesting feature of digital texts is the ability to assign appropriate books to individual students through virtual bookshelves using tools such as Scholastic's Storia. Tools like Storia allow the teacher to create individualized bookshelves with only the books that the teacher has selected for the student. This feature ensures that the student is reading books that are appropriate for his or her reading level. Even more useful, with tools like Folletshelf (www.aboutfollettebooks.com/follettshelf.cfm), teachers can assign a particular order for books to be read, can insert questions and comments into books using a notes feature, and can provide, within the text, links to resources that would be helpful for individual students. These virtual bookshelves promote even more individualized attention to each student, while also keeping their designated books personal and private as students each have their own bookshelf.

Helping Students Select Texts Suitable for Their Reading Levels

Whether you use Lexile levels, Guided Reading levels, or some other book leveling system, it is sometimes difficult to determine the reading level of books your students want to read, especially when it comes to digital books, because they are not marked with a special coding system as many classroom books are. However, there are ways to manage this obstacle. One option is to use an app such as Level It Books for tablets and smart phones. This app allows the user to scan the bar code of books to view Lexile, Guided Reading, Grade Level Equivalent, and Developmental Reading Assessment levels for the book. Or, the user can quickly find these levels for digital books by typing in the title. This app also acts as a check out system so that teachers can track what students are reading and make appropriate recommendations accordingly, creating an efficient and organized library system personalized to your classroom.

A SAMPLE LESSON PLAN

In this final section of the chapter we provide a sample lesson plan (see Table 3.1) to illustrate ways of using digital books to teach both digital and non-digital literacy skills. This lesson plan was developed using the instructional planning cycle presented in chapter 2 and should act as a guide in planning your own lesson with the cycle. Although this lesson plan is based on Third Grade Common Core Standards, it could easily be adapted for most grade levels. In this lesson, students will be doing a close reading of a digital text about a science topic and identifying main ideas and supporting details in the text, will be responding to questions about the text and providing evidence from the text to support their answers, and will be determining the meaning of several science-specific words. Students will use the Diigo app or website to highlight important details in the text and insert notes to answer questions

Table 3.1.   Third Grade Sample Lesson Plan on Learning With Digital Books

Instructional Goals of the lesson:
- Students will be able to read a digital book and answer questions to demonstrate their understanding of the text, referring explicitly to the text as the basis for the answers by using Diigo (www.diigo.com) to insert digital sticky notes where they find their answers.
- Students will determine the meaning of domain-specific words and phrases, using contextual clues and illustrations, and will use Diigo to insert notes explaining the meaning of the words.
- Students will identify the main idea of text selections and recount the key details that support the main idea using Diigo highlighting and sticky note tools.
- Students will digitally share their Diigo annotations with a partner and digitally discuss their agreement or disagreement on the meaning of domain-specific words and the main ideas of the text selections.
- Students will work with partners to post the information they learned on their topic to a class blog. All students will discuss their ideas about each group's posts on the blog.

Common Core Standards Addressed:
CCSS.ELA-LITERACY.RI.3.1
Ask and answer questions to demonstrate understanding of a text, referring explicitly to the text as the basis for the answers.
CCSS.ELA-LITERACY.RI.3.2
Determine the main idea of a text; recount the key details and explain how they support the main idea.
CCSS.ELA-LITERACY.RI.3.4
Determine the meaning of general academic and domain-specific words and phrases in a text relevant to a grade 3 topic or subject area.
CCSS.ELA-LITERACY.W.3.6
With guidance and support from adults, use technology to produce and publish writing (using keyboarding skills) as well as to interact and collaborate with others.

English Language Proficiency Standards Addressed:
1. Construct meaning from oral presentations and literary and informational text through grade-appropriate listening, reading, and viewing
2. Participate in grade-appropriate oral and written exchanges of information, ideas, and analyses, responding to peer, audience, or reader comments and questions
3. Speak and write about grade-appropriate complex literary and informational texts and topics
4. Construct grade-appropriate oral and written claims and support them with reasoning and evidence
6. Analyze and critique the arguments of others orally and in writing
8. Determine the meaning of words and phrases in oral presentations and literary and informational text
10. Make accurate use of standard English to communicate in grade-appropriate speech and writing

Lesson Description & Instructional Approach:
1. Go to www.wegivebooks.org to find online informational books that are appropriate for your students to read. Students will be working in pairs for this assignment. We recommend assigning several different books on the same topic to different students so that students will see a wide variety of perspectives when they later share their information with each other.
2. Provide students with a list of questions based on the text. These questions should guide the students in comprehending the text and in identifying the main ideas of the text. Have students use the sticky note feature of the Diigo toolbar (www.diigo.com) to insert their answers to the questions and show where they found the answer in the text.
3. Ask students to identify the meaning of domain-specific vocabulary words that you have identified for them by inserting a digital sticky note where they find the term in the text. Students should provide their own definition of the word based on the context and add their definition to the digital sticky note (see Figure 3.4).
4. On the final page of each section of the text (or sections selected by the teacher), students should identify the main idea of the text section and identify key details and explain how they support the main idea. Students should insert a digital sticky note with this information at the end of each section. Students can use the highlighter feature to highlight key details within the text.
5. Students should then share the sticky notes on which they defined the vocabulary terms and the main ideas in the text with another student in the class who read the same book. Students can share these digitally by using the share feature on Diigo (see Figure 3.5). Because the notes are available digitally, students can also collaborate on this assignment by sharing them with students in other classes. Students should then discuss whether they agree with their partner's definitions and determination of the main ideas and details. Students should insert digital sticky notes to explain why they agree or disagree with their partner's information.
6. Finally, partners should collaborate to write a blog post describing the main ideas of each section of the text and identifying important domain-specific vocabulary. Have each set of partners publish their findings to a class blog (we recommend www.kidblog.org). Students in the class can read each other's posts to learn more about the topic. The teacher should then lead a class discussion on the topic and discuss how different books offered different information and clarify any conflicting information or confusing aspects of the topic.

(continued)

Table 3.1.   (*continued*)

Digital Tools, Site, and Apps Used:
1. Book website: www.wegivebooks.org
2. Diigo text annotation and sharing tools (go to www.diigo.com to create an account and place the digital annotation tools in the toolbar).
3. Blogging tool: www.kidblog.org

Digital Contribution to Instruction:
- Using the free book site provides free access to books that might not be available in the classroom and helps students learn how to navigate a digital text.
- Using Diigo allows students to annotate the book and leave notes that can be saved and accessed later.
- Diigo allows students to share their work both in and out of the classroom and provides unique possibilities for collaboration.
- Posting work to the class blog provides a space for discussion that can be accessed asynchronously and both in and out of the classroom.

Potential Constraints:
- Accounts for Diigo and Kidblog will need to be set up in advance. The teacher will need to consider if students will have their own Diigo accounts or share a class account. Signing into individual accounts may be difficult and time-consuming. The teacher should carefully plan how to handle this aspect of instruction.

Instructional Considerations:
- The teacher will need to ensure that he or she is able to access all students' digital sticky notes.
- The teacher may need to create a master list of student login information for the websites, depending on whether students use a shared class account or have individual accounts.
- The teacher may need to facilitate the online discussion or provide guidelines, depending on how familiar students are with this type of discussion.

Reflection
After conducting the lesson, consider the extent to which you were able to adhere to your instructional goal. What helped or hindered your students' abilities to meet the instructional goal? Note what you may need to do differently the next time you use these technologies.

and identify key ideas. They will then collaborate with digital partners by sharing and discussing their annotations and posting information they have learned to a class blog.

RESOURCES

Given how rapidly new apps and websites emerge, it would be impossible to provide a comprehensive, or even thorough, list of resources related to the

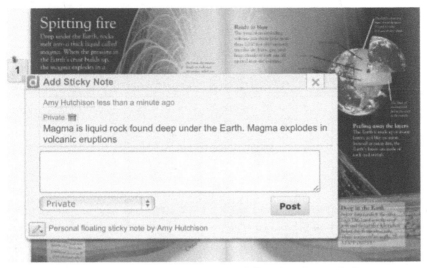

Figure 3.4.   Sticky note created with Diigo to define domain vocabulary.

Figure 3.5.   Screenshot of notes that will be shared with a partner.

Table 3.2. Resources and Sample Activities for Reading Digital Texts

Digital Resources	Possible Uses	Grade-Specific Examples & CCSS Addressed
E-readers: • iPad* (Apple-iBooks app) • Kindle (Amazon) • Nook (Barnes & Noble) *Note that tablets such as iPads allow e-reading apps for devices such as Kindle and Nook to be downloaded onto the tablet so that books purchased with a Kindle or Nook are also available to be read on the tablet.	Students may: • Navigate and search text for key features such as main ideas and supporting statements • Annotate text and make notes about reading, such as plot, thematic or character connections or observations • Support/enhance reading with audio text-to-speech features • Develop vocabulary through dictionary features	Fifth-grade students may read an e-reader book, and with a partner, make notes using the keyboard and annotation features to consider a character's motivation in fiction. **CCSS.ELA-Literacy.RL.5.2:** *Determine a theme of a story, drama, or poem from details in the text, including how characters in a story or drama respond to challenges or how the speaker in a poem reflects upon a topic; summarize the text.* Second-grade students may read a digital story or book and use annotation and highlighting features to locate the main idea of the text. **CCSS.ELA-Literacy.RI.2.2:** *Identify the main topic of a multiparagraph text as well as the focus of specific paragraphs within the text.* Third-grade students may use the built-in dictionary features of an e-reader to read an informational text with abstract or unfamiliar language. **CCSS.ELA-Literacy.RI.3.4:** *Determine the meaning of general academic and domain-specific words and phrases in a text relevant to a grade 3 topic or subject area.*

Kindergarteners may view stories and picture books using a storybook app that provides visual images and interactive elements and audio features and retell the story after viewing.
CCSS.ELA-Literacy.RL.K.2: *With prompting and support, retell familiar stories, including key details.*

Fourth-grade students may analyze a print and digital version of *The Tale of Peter Rabbit* to compare story elements in the two versions
CCSS.ELA-Literacy.RL.4.7: *Make connections between the text of a story or drama and a visual or oral presentation of the text, identifying where each version reflects specific descriptions and directions in the text.*

Have third-grade students read an informational text and use Evernote to create voice notes and text annotations within the text to share and compare with a partner who read the same text
CCSS.ELA-Literacy.W.3.6: *With guidance and support from adults, use technology to produce and publish writing (using keyboarding skills) as well as to interact and collaborate with others.*

First-graders may listen to a story read aloud and explain to a partner, teacher, or through drawing which character is speaking at various points in the story.
CCSS.ELA-Literacy.RL.1.6: *Identify who is telling the story at various points in a text.*

Students may:
- Use graphics, audio, and read-to-me or story playback features to engage in reading
- Read texts in multiple formats (e.g., words, visuals, audio) to improve comprehension
- Compare print-based stories to digitally interactive stories for understanding
- Use touch features to sound out or replay words or phrases
- Support comprehension with interactive visuals to enhance reading
- Use social bookmarking to annotate and also share annotations

Students may:
- Find and use supplemental texts for comparison to class texts
- Navigate online texts to select readings
- Listen to stories read aloud by authors and celebrities

Apps:
- iBooks
- Storia by Scholastic
- Diigo
- Evernote
- GoodReader
- Subtext
- PaperPort Notes
- Storybook apps
  - *Jack and the Beanstalk*
  - *Green Eggs and Ham*
  - *Bartleby's Book of Buttons*
  - *Alice for iPad*
  - *Popout! The Tale of Peter Rabbit*

Online Book Resources:
- Free books on Unite for Literacy (www.uniteforliteracy.com)
- *Online Story Time* by Barnes & Noble (www.barnesandnoble.com)
- We Give Books (www.wegivebooks.org)
- Follett Shelf (www.aboutfollettbooks.com)

content of this chapter. Therefore, we have instead selected some representative resources that you might use for each type of classroom activity described in the previous sections. Table 3.2 provides a sampling of resources and illustrates the types of activities for which they might be used. In this table we have also made specific connections to the Common Core State Standards to illustrate how both digital and non-digital standards can be addressed with these tools. Our hope is that the brief descriptions provided in this table will help you to begin thinking about ways to integrate digital reading into your classroom and help you to see the many ways that digital texts can be used to support literacy learning for students of all ages.

REFLECTION QUESTIONS

1. Consider the many forms of digital text that you have read. How did you interact with the text differently than when you read a paper-based book or document? Did you take advantage of digital features, such as a built-in dictionary or the ability to copy and paste text to make notes? Why or why not?
2. Consider what would make you more likely to take advantage of the features of a digital text. How can you support your students in learning how to navigate digital texts and take advantage of the many features of digital texts that can support readers? Make a plan to teach students how to use the features of digital texts.

REFERENCES

Bates, C. C. (2013). How do wii know: Anecdotal records go digital. *The Reading Teacher, 67*(1), 25–29.

Booth, D. W. (2006). *Reading doesn't matter anymore: Shattering the myths of literacy*. Portland, ME: Stenhouse.

Kunhardt, D. (1962). *Pat the bunny.* Racine, WI: Golden Press.

Lankshear, C., & Knobel, M. (2011). *New literacies: Everyday practices and classroom learning* (3rd ed.). Maidenhead, UK: Open University Press.

Larson, L. C. (2010). Digital Readers: The Next Chapter in E-Book Reading and Response. *The Reading Teacher, 64*(1), 15–22. doi:10.1598/RT.64.1.2

Rosenblatt, L.M. (1968). *Literature as exploration* (2nd ed). New York: Noble and Noble.

Suess, Dr. (1960). *Green eggs and ham.* New York: Random House.

Suess, Dr. (1957). *The cat in the hat.* Boston: Houghton Mifflin.

Zhang, S., Duke, N., & Jimenez, L. (2011). The WWWDOT approach to improving students' critical evaluation of websites. *The Reading Teacher, 65*(2), 150–58.

Chapter Four

Using Digital Images
in the Classroom

Last month, Mrs. Johnson was successful in helping her students learn how to navigate and use the features of digital books and some types of websites. She is proud of the progress her students have made and believes they are ready to learn some new skills. However, despite the progress her students have made, she and her students faced challenges when trying out the new technology tools Mrs. Johnson introduced. One challenge was that the students started working on their text annotation using the Diigo app on iPads from the shared cart available for checkout. However, they did not complete their work on the first day and needed to continue it in class the next day. Unfortunately, the iPads were not available for checkout the following day. After consulting with some fellow teachers, Mrs. Johnson discovered that, because the students had been using a tool that requires students to sign into an account (Diigo), their work could be opened and continued on a computer or a different digital device even though they had originally started the work on the iPads. She is pleased to learn of this flexibility and has learned an important lesson; it is helpful to use tools that can be accessed on different types of devices. Otherwise, she should have a plan in place for how students can continue their work if they don't finish on the first day.

This month, Mrs. Johnson's literacy coach has introduced a new tool called Thinglink, which helps make images interactive by allowing the user to embed videos, notes, and music into pictures or drawings. Mrs. Johnson is excited about integrating this new app because she can see many ways that it can potentially support the literacy goals that she has developed for her students based on the Common Core State Standards. Having her students begin to use images to convey their understanding also aligns with her long-range plan for integrating technology. Therefore, this month she will have her students use the Thinglink app to create drawings that integrate text and video to show their understanding of story elements. She plans a lesson that integrates Thinglink using the Technology Integration Planning Cycle for Literacy and Language Arts (see Figure 2.1 in Chapter 2). As she plans her lesson she realizes that students must sign into an account to use the tool. However, Thinglink can be used on both computers and iPads and continued on either device, regardless of where they began the work. Although creating accounts for the students will take extra time, she realizes that this require-ment is beneficial because students can do their work on both computers and iPads. That way, students can work on the computers and iPads that she has in her classroom during their independent work time and can continue on whatever device is available during their next independent work session.

Teachers often ask students to study images and pictures in print-based books to gather additional information or to make sense of the written content of books or other texts. Teachers may also instruct students to "close your eyes and imagine" when reading a story so that they may visualize what an author is describing and better comprehend information. Similarly, students are asked to visualize themselves or someone they know in situations read about in written text to consider perspective. Further, when we incorporate pictorial images from history, such as photographs or drawings, into class-room instruction for students to consider images, we ask them to consider context and different aspects of the images. In doing so, students both read and analyze images as text. When we ask students to engage in these types of activities, we ultimately ask our students to read images or to create images based on reading. These types of activities allow our students to build com-prehension skills, hone analysis techniques, and participate in visual literacy to understand a text, idea, event, or topic. In this way, we engage our students in multiliteracies (Anstey & Bull, 2006; New London Group, 1996) to con-sider various forms of personal, social, and cultural knowledge and engage in reading practices that span different types of texts (e.g., written and graphic). Additionally, as Hobbs and Moore (2013) note, "Today, people need to be able to 'read' and 'write' messages using symbols in a variety of forms" (p. 15). Images are one of the symbols with which our students must be literate in reading and writing to be digital citizens in today's world.

Written text and images have always been interdependent, either through images accompanying text (e.g., picture books) or through written text meant to evoke images through vivid description (e.g., descriptive poetry or fiction). Yet, the onset of digital technology has expanded the potential to read and also write a variety of texts using digital images. For example, images and videos of farm workers on a website focused on Cesar Chavez and civil rights may be considered the sole text for a lesson, and students must be taught how to read these types of text for comprehension. Teachers may also find rich areas for classroom discussion and activities by pausing media during play and having students consider the frozen image and the frame for analysis (Hobbs & Moore, 2013). Additionally, students could respond to reading by creating or altering images using digital cameras, apps, or Internet tools, which may promote more intricate and complex responses as digital tools afford many students opportunities for creating rich images as opposed to paper drawings. By having students respond to readings using multiple literacies entailed in producing images or digital drawings created from a number of digital aspects (e.g., colors, framing, size, shading, etc.) offered by production tools, students may be better equipped to apply what they have learned in new and meaningful ways, or through transformed practice (New London Group, 1996).

COMMON CORE CONNECTIONS

Using digital images in K-6 classrooms are also supported by the CCSS. Using the previous example of a website to have students consider civil rights and the role of Cesar Chavez in the movement, students may examine the images to determine central ideas or themes of a text and summarize key details and ideas (CCSS.ELA-LITERACY.CCRA.R.2). Upper-elementary students could also "assess how point of view or purpose shapes the content and style of a text" (CCSS.ELA-LITERACY.CCRA.R.6). Further, when considering the new literacies involved with using digital technology, we must reconsider what writing looks like in a digital format. An image produced by students in response to a text or to capture an idea may indeed be considered writing as it is a medium of communication to portray an idea. Thus, not only would students use technology to produce and publish writing (CCSS.ELA-LITERACY.CCRA.W.6), they could also "write informative or explanatory texts to examine and convey complex ideas and information clearly and accurately through the effective selection, organization, and analysis of content" (CCSS.ELA-LITERACY.CCRA.W.1). Such examples again show how CCSS standards that do not explicitly address technology are addressed through the integration of digital tools into classroom literacy instruction.

The next section introduces multiple methods for using and incorporating digital images into your instruction. We encourage you to reflect on your own classroom as you read about these uses and even adapt or modify our suggestions. Think about ways that you already use images in your classroom and how the learning opportunities offered by images might be expanded as you move to helping your students read and produce digital images.

USING DIGITAL IMAGES IN THE CLASSROOM

Annotating Photos or Web Images

Annotating photos and other web images can be a valuable activity for demonstrating understanding. For example, a teacher could have students annotate images found in a digital picture book to show information they gained from looking at the illustrations or photos. Alternately, websites often consist of as many, or more, images as text. Therefore, it is important that students are able to correctly interpret those images. Teachers can guide students in understanding how to read those images through annotation. Students can digitally draw or write on top of images found online to show that they understand the meaning or to draw attention to important parts of the image. There are many digital tools that allow students to annotate images, and it is particularly easy to do on tablets since they are operated through a touch screen. Skitch is an example of an annotation tool that is available as a tablet app or can be used on a computer. Skitch allows the user to annotate images from the camera role or captured from the web. Visit http://evernote.com/skitch/ to learn more about Skitch and see examples of annotated images.

Using Digital Images to Respond to Fiction and Non-fiction Texts

Students can respond to texts and demonstrate their understanding of a text by creating digital images. This can be done in several ways. First, students may create their own illustrations to show how they are interpreting a particular text after reading it. For example, after reading an informational text about clouds, students could draw and label a type of cloud to illustrate their understanding (see Figure 4.1 for a screenshot of a sample drawing completed with Doodle Buddy).

Although this simple activity could also be done with pencil and paper, by using a digital tool such as the tablet app Doodle Buddy, students are learning how to use a digital tool and the images that are created can be saved to the tablet camera roll and used later or inserted as an image into another app. Additionally, in a classroom study, Hutchison, Beschorner & Schmidt-Crawford (2012) found that students reported being more attentive to the details of their work and more likely to correct wrong details when drawing on a tablet as opposed to drawing with pencil and paper.

Students can also use their visualization skills to create images prior to reading. In a fourth grade classroom study, Hutchison, Beschorner & Schmidt-Crawford (2012) had groups of students visualize and create an image to go with a portion of text prior to reading the whole text. Each group of

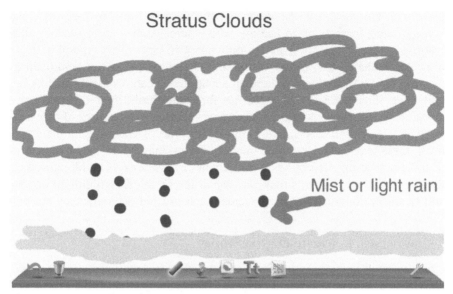

Figure 4.1. Screenshot of Doodle Buddy drawing.

students was assigned a different portion of text and each group shared and explained their images with the class in the story order. This way, students had heard about the story and seen accompanying images before reading the story. This activity served to activate the students' prior knowledge on the topic, provided an opportunity to discuss any confusing vocabulary terms, and provided an opportunity to clarify any misconceptions prior to reading. During this activity, students spent much time changing the details of their pictures to accurately portray the text. For example, one group of students had been assigned a portion of text about a flimsy bridge. The students first had to determine the meaning of the word flimsy in order to know how to draw the bridge. The students then revised the bridge several times in order to make it look flimsy. Accordingly, this activity provided a way for the teacher to know that the students understood the meaning of the text and provided a reason for the students to discuss the meaning of words they did not understand.

Using Images to Build Informational Texts

Drawing and capturing images are also beneficial activities for non-fiction texts. Students can learn more about the purpose of non-fiction text features by creating their own informational visuals. For example, students can draw their own maps, diagrams, and tables. We find the screenshot capture function of iPads, tablets, and computers particularly useful when having students learn with Google Earth. Students can use Google Earth to seek different types of land formations to capture with a screenshot then use to describe features of geography they are learning about in class. This type of activity indicates students' knowledge of not only the key aspects of a land feature, but also their knowledge of where on a map these features are located. After collecting screenshot images, students may then build their own informational texts (e.g., a book about plateaus or geographical features of a desert) to share with classmates or add to the class library. Depending on the grade level, these texts may be simple images, or they may be advanced diagrams of images accompanied by text to highlight key features. If highlighting key features with text, students may also use different colors to highlight important words or domain specific vocabulary and to label diagrams they create.

Using Images to Create Digital Stories

Once students know how to create and save images, they can use those images to create digital stories. Simply put, digital storytelling is the practice of using digital tools to combine images, and often audio, video, and web publishing, to tell a story. There are numerous apps and websites that facilitate digital storytelling to make the technical aspects simple. Making students' stories digital may be the simplest aspect of digital storytelling. The more challenging part is guiding students in how to create meaningful stories from an effective point of view, how to create an appropriate tone, and how to use music effectively. Those aspects of digital storytelling must be addressed through instruction. There are storyboarding apps, such as Felt Board or Comic Life, that can help students plan their stories by placing images and text in the order they would like them to appear and adding notes about the digital story. Students can then use a storytelling tool to publish their stories. Students can use their own drawings or photographs for their stories, or use images from an open source such as Flickr (www.Flickr.com), which allows users to copy images as long as credit is given to the source.

Constructing Class Books with Photos and Illustrations

Another way that you can have students use digital images is for constructing a digital class book that can be shared with an outside audience. There are many kinds of books that could be created. However, we like that the built-in camera feature of tablets such as iPads allows students to easily capture things in their environment. One example of a book that could be created is with a first grade classroom's study of punctuation marks. Students could walk around the classroom with iPads to find and photograph examples of each type of punctuation in their environment. Students could then discuss and write about all the different places they found each punctuation mark and how it was used. They could then combine their images into a digital book using the app My Story-Book Maker (www.mystoryapp.org) and share the book by posting it to the class blog and tweeting a link to it through their class Twitter account. The My Story-Book Maker app also allows teachers to create a class account that will allow each child to have their own bookshelf of stories. This type of activity, when conducted with a mobile device, allows students to find things in their authentic environments and create a collection of related ideas that can help them better understand a concept.

Teaching Students How to Read Images

Teachers know the importance of helping students learn how to make sense of the pictures and illustrations found in storybooks since those images add to the meaning of the text. The same is true with digital images, though digital images occur in a variety of contexts much broader than storybooks. For example, digital books may contain interactive images that allow the user to manipulate the image in some way or link the reader to an activity, another website, a definition or explanation and more. Additionally, websites may contain photos, illustrations, videos, and icons that the reader must interpret. Therefore it is critical that teachers teach students how to make meaning from these images. This type of teaching can begin as simply as asking students to try to determine what is happening, or the main idea, in a digital image in which the main idea would be fairly clear. From there, you could guide students in making inferences based on the image, requiring them to describe the specific aspects of the image that support their inferences. You could compare students' responses to illustrate the many different interpretations and ideas that can come from an image. By conducting these activities, you would build on students' print-based literacy skills, and therefore support their abilities to read both digital and non-digital text.

Another way to guide students in reading images is to have them write a detailed description of everything they see in a selected image and annotate the image to make sure they have noticed everything in the photo or image. Students will know that they have noticed all aspects of the image when each feature of the image has an annotation. For young students, teachers may want to first point out the different features of the image or instruct students to annotate a certain number of features. Once students become proficient at reading images in isolation, it will be important to then guide them in reading

---

Textbox 4.1.

Focus On:
Safely Locating Images

Challenge: Many elementary teachers express concern about having young students search for and locate images on the Internet as they may come across inappropriate websites in their search. Teachers also worry that students will become overwhelmed with the vast amount of images available on photo-sharing sites, such as Flickr, and become discouraged or distracted when working with digital images to build text.

Consider: Education-focused search tools or digital closed-networks built by you or other teachers to store resources for your students to access.

Strategies:
1. For younger (K-2) elementary students, host a Google+ or class blog space where you have located and stored images for students to search, eliminating web searches.
2. For older (3–6) elementary students, provide quick, 10-minute mini-lessons with modeling to review Internet search and safety rules prior to lessons involving digital image location.
3. If using a photo-sharing site, provide students with specific search terms that you have already vetted prior to the lesson.
4. Have students brainstorm ideas for images they would like to find and use to map out their text before beginning a search.
5. Pair students together, and make one student the searcher, who locates images online, and one the moderator, who checks proper search procedure and guidelines (using a teacher-generated check list) to hold their partner accountable while searching.

Check Out: *Sweet Search* (www.sweetsearch.com/)

Sweet Search is a kid-friendly search engine that has been evaluated by experts for use by children and provides a more limited and safe search engine for students to find images and online information.

---

images as they are found in digital environments. As previously mentioned, a single website can contain many different types of images that serve different functions and are likely to be noticed and read in a non-linear fashion. It is important to help students understand how to read all of these images that occur together but serve different functions and guide the reader in varying ways. We highlight methods for helping students safely locate images in the Focus box below (see Textbox 4.1).

*Students use ppt to create an book
ABC*

SAMPLE LESSON PLAN

The lesson in Table 4.1 involves the use of Thinglink and Doodle Buddy. Thinglink is free for educators and can be used on both computers and tablets. Thinglink allows the user to make images interactive by adding music, video, text, and even polls to an image. Visit www.thinglink.com to learn more, http://bit.ly/1ja67Mj for a tutorial on using Thinglink, or http://bit.ly/1ja6tCM for a step-by-step guide to using Thinglink. Doodle Buddy is a drawing app that is also free. The example in Table 4.1 describes a lesson in which students use the Doodle Buddy app to create images that show their understanding of story characters, settings, and events. Students then further explain their understanding by making the image interactive using the Thinglink app to embed relevant videos, text, and photos. This sample lesson is conducted with iPads. However, it could also be adapted for computers and could easily be adapted for multiple grade levels by increasing the complexity of the information students must provide in response to the story.

RESOURCES

Table 4.2 highlights different types of digital resources useful to incorporating images into classroom instruction. This table presents examples of digital tools that may be used for integrating digital images, broad ideas about integrating digital images into your instruction, and also a specific example of using digital images in instruction for each K-6 grade level. Consider how you may adapt some of these broad ideas or transfer the specific examples to the grade level you teach.

REFLECTION QUESTIONS

1. Consider how much the illustrations in picture books contribute to the meaning of a story. How can you use your students' familiarity with picture books to help them understand the extent and variety of information they can convey with drawings and photographs and to help them understand the importance of choosing the right colors and design to convey their message?
2. What are the advantages of creating images digitally?
3. How can making an image interactive change the message of the picture?
4. For what learning situations or activities would it best be to have students create digital images instead of non-digital images? How about non-digital images instead of digital images?

Table 4.1.   Sample Second Grade Lesson Plan Using Thinglink to Illustrate Story Elements

Instructional Goals of the lesson:
Students will use Thinglink, Doodle Buddy, and images found on the web to demonstrate their understanding of story characters, settings, and events.

Common Core Standards Addressed:
CCSS.ELA-LITERACY.RL.2.7
Use information gained from the illustrations and words in a print or digital text to demonstrate understanding of its characters, setting, or plot.
CCSS.ELA-LITERACY.W.2.6
With guidance and support from adults, use a variety of digital tools to produce and publish writing, including in collaboration with peers.
CCSS.ELA-LITERACY.SL.2.5
Create audio recordings of stories or poems; add drawings or other visual displays to stories or recounts of experiences when appropriate to clarify ideas, thoughts, and feelings.
CCSS.ELA-LITERACY.RL.2.10
By the end of the year, read and comprehend literature, including stories and poetry, in the grades 2-3 text complexity band proficiently, with scaffolding as needed at the high end of the range.

English Language Proficiency Standards Addressed:
1. Construct meaning from oral presentations and literary and informational text through grade-appropriate listening, reading, and viewing
3. Speak and write about grade-appropriate complex literary and informational texts and topics
1. Speak and write about grade-appropriate complex literary and informational texts and topics

Lesson Description & Instructional Approach:
- After reading a story, students will be guided in determining the characters, settings, and events in a story.
- Students will demonstrate their understanding of the characters, settings, and events by creating a Thinglink image (www.thinglink.com) on the iPad following the steps below:
  ° Using the Doodle Buddy app, students will draw an illustration of the characters, settings, and/or events in the story and save it to the iPad camera roll.
  ° Students will open the Thinglink app and import the Doodle Buddy illustration that was saved to the camera roll.
  ° Students will add one sentence to the illustration to further describe the character, settings or events by tapping the illustration, selecting "add text," and typing the sentence.
  ° Students will add one video to further illustrate the character, settings or events by tapping the illustration, selecting "add media" and "add from Youtube," and then searching for a video to support their work.

- ° Students will add one image to their illustration by first searching the web using key words. For example, if the student is looking for an image to go with a main character named Farmer Bill, they would search images using the key word farmer. Students will then save the image to the camera roll and add it to their illustration by tapping it and selecting "add media" and "choose from gallery" to insert the image they saved to the camera roll.
- ° Students will share their image by selecting the email icon to email to the teacher or selecting the Twitter icon to share it to the class Twitter page.

Note: See Figures 4.4-4.5 for an example of a ThingLink created for this lesson. Visit http://www.thinglink.com/scene/517732634181238786 to see the interactive image online.

Digital Tools/apps Used:
- Doodle Buddy app for iPad
- Thinglink app for iPad
- Web browser for searching
- YouTube

Digital Contribution to Instruction:
- Using Thinglink provides students with multiple ways to demonstrate their understanding of story elements and provides them with an opportunity to learn how to create a multimodal text.
- Using these tools provides students with practice searching for information on the web with a simple activity in a controlled setting.
- Images saved to the camera roll can be used again later for other related activities for the story.
- Students learn how multiple forms of text can be combined to explain an idea.
- Students gain experience using digital tools to publish their writing.

Potential Constraints:
- Students may have difficulty switching between apps. **Solution:** This could be solved by carefully demonstrating how to switch between apps and explaining that the videos and images they will insert can be opened within Thinglink. Students do not need to exit the Thinglink app to add images, video, or sentences to their illustration.
- Students may have difficulty finding images or video to support their illustration. **Solution:** The teacher can help students with this by explaining how to use simple keyword searches and providing examples.

Instructional Considerations:
- Thinglink requires the user to sign into an account. However, once signed into Thinglink on the iPad the user remains signed in. The teacher will need to consider if she will sign into Thinglink on all of the iPads or provide students with the account information and have them sign in.

Reflection:
After conducting the lesson, consider the extent to which you were able to adhere to your instructional goal. What helped or hindered your students' abilities to meet the instructional goal? Note what you may need to do differently the next time you use these technologies.

Table 4.2. Resources and Sample Activities for Using Digital Images in the Classroom

Digital Resources	Possible Uses	Grade-Specific Examples & CCSS Addressed
Digital Tools: • iPad/Tablet Camera • Digital Camera	Students may: • Capture images to illustrate words, colors, or shapes • Take pictures that represent ideas from a story • Create a story sequence Teachers may: • Create story maps or timelines to outline units. • Use pictorial prompts to promote and guide student writing.	With the help of a teacher, second-grade students may create tableaus representing scenes from a created story, and capture tableaus with an iPad camera to create a story sequence. This activity may be expanded to have students write captions or annotations on the pictures using an annotation iPad app. **CCSS.ELA-LITERACY.W.2.3:** *Write narratives in which they recount a well-elaborated event or short sequence of events, include details to describe actions, thoughts, and feelings, use temporal words to signal event order, and provide a sense of closure.* With the assistance of a teacher, kindergarten students may orally tell a biographical story and use images to support this retelling. **CCSS.ELA.LITERACY.RL.K.2:** *With prompting and support, retell familiar stories, including key details.*

Fourth-grade students may use a drawing app to depict characters from a story to compare and contrast character traits.

CCSS.ELA-LITERACY.RL.5.3: *Compare and contrast two or more characters, settings, or events in a story or drama, drawing on specific details in the text (e.g., how characters interact).*

Sixth-grade students may capture and annotate different geographic forms (i.e., rivers, lakes, basins) to show comprehension of informational texts, such as maps.

CCSS.ELA-LITERACY.RI.6.7: *Integrate information presented in different media or formats (e.g., visually, quantitatively) as well as in words to develop a coherent understanding of a topic or issue.*

Third-grade students may use an app to animate or add text to images of early explorers to describe important aspects of that explorer and their contributions to history.

CCSS.ELA-LITERACY.W.3.2: *Write informative/explanatory texts to examine a topic and convey ideas and information clearly.*

CCSS.ELA.LITERACY.W.3.2.A: *Introduce a topic and group related information together; include illustrations when useful to aiding comprehension.*

CCSS.ELA-LITERACY.W.3.2B: *Develop the topic with facts, definitions, and details.*

(continued)

Students may:
- Use drawing tools to summarize or retell the plot of a story or depict character traits
- Use storytelling tools to draw/create a fiction or nonfiction text
- Capture screenshots to illustrate different geographical landscapes represented in fiction and nonfiction texts [ELA/Geography connection]
- Use images to illustrate their written text to develop fiction or nonfiction books
- Use effects to animate or add text to photos

Teachers may:
- Develop digital field trips for students to consider various topics in history and science.
- Support struggling readers by incorporating images with text to promote comprehension.

Apps:
- Doodle Buddy
- MyStory
- Google Earth
- Book Creator
- FotoFlexer
- Thinglink
- Skitch
- Felt Board
- Comic Life
- You Doodle
- PhotoPen
- Snap Camera!
- iDraw
- SimpleDraw
- Inkflow Visual Notebook

Table 4.2. (continued)

Digital Resources	Possible Uses	Grade-Specific Examples & CCSS Addressed
Online Resources: • Picnik Photobucket • Flickr (also has an app) • Wylio • Foto Tagger	Students may: • Create a postcard in the perspective of a fiction character or historical figure [ELA/History connection] • Explore photos to create a collage to depict or explain an important event described in a text • Embed images in a blog to illustrate a digital diary of an important life event Teachers may: • Create classroom collages to summarize learning from units. • Illustrate class blogs with images for parents to view.	With the assistance of a teacher, first-grade students may create a visual depiction of the setting of a story or book using photo-sharing online resources to find and select photos to create a collage or another type of display that would depict a setting. **CCSS.ELA-LITERACY.RL.1.3:** *Describe characters, settings, and major events in a story, using key details.*

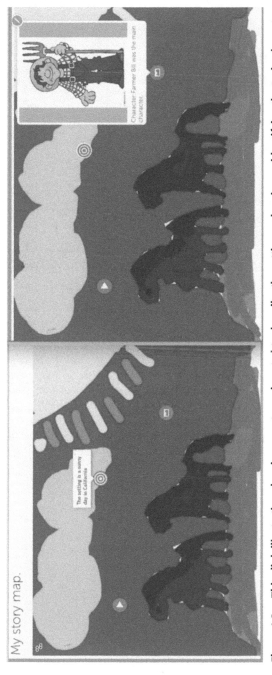

Figure 4.2. Thinglink illustration showing a sentence inserted to describe the setting and an image identifying the main character.

Figure 4.3. Thinglink illustration showing a video inserted to demonstrate a problem in the story.

REFERENCES

Anstey, M., & Bull, G. (2006). *Teaching and learning multiliteracies: Changing times, changing literacies.* International Reading Association.

Hobbs, R., & Moore, D.C. (2013). *Discovering media literacy: Teaching digital media and popular culture in elementary school.* Thousand Oaks, CA: Sage.

New London Group. (1996). A pedagogy of multiliteracies: Designing social futures. *Harvard Educational Review, 66*(1), 60–92.

Chapter Five

Using Digital Audio Tools
in the Classroom

Last month, Mrs. Johnson's students successfully used the Thinglink app to create interactive images relating to the story elements of books they were reading. Her students enjoyed the activity and were successful at identifying the story elements and illustrating them with the app. They even shared their Thinglink images on their class blog and shared links to them through Twitter so that their families and friends could learn about what they were reading. Now that Mrs. Johnson's students are familiar with reading digital texts and creating digital images, she is ready to continue introducing new digital skills and tools. This month she will introduce some digital audio recording tools that can be used in a variety of ways. Her instructional coach has shown her ways of using three apps for audio recording: Evernote, Voice Recorder, and My Story-Book Maker. Therefore, she will introduce these apps to her students. However, she wants to be sure that students continue to practice the skills they have already learned, so she will also incorporate images and have her students search for information online. You can see in Table 5.1 how Mrs. Johnson chose to combine these tools to help her students write an explanatory text about a science topic. As Mrs. Johnson planned her lesson, she realized that combining several different digital tools may be confusing for her students. Therefore, she was able to consider how she might break up the lesson so that it could be presented over several different class periods and she could introduce one tool at a time. Using this approach worked well and her students did not become overwhelmed by the tools. She was pleased that she thought of this potential difficulty in advance and was able to prevent her students from becoming overwhelmed by their task.

Digital audio tools and features have changed the landscape of literacy in classroom instruction. Kress (2003) contends that printed page text is no longer the primary mode of communication or expression and students must learn to read and write using multiple forms of communication, as digital tools, such as podcasts and audio recording, make it easier to communicate with sound and video, in addition to print-based text. Audio tools also provide opportunities for students to enhance their reading and writing experiences through listening to supplementary audio to support textual reading and producing audio to increase comprehension of text. The benefits of added audio features to the K-6 classroom are not new. Reading a book aloud or playing an audio recording of a reading or song are typical instructional practices found in many classrooms. It is also common to hear students engage in a choral reading or read aloud to one another or the class. Indeed, practices such as read-alouds are common because they improve students' comprehension using audio to support and promote learning (International Reading Association & National Association for the Education of Young Children, 1998; Snow, Burns, & Griffin, 1998). However, digital audio tools can provide even more opportunities for supporting students as they learn to read increasingly complex texts.

The use of digital audio tools in instruction builds on these traditional practices to support and enhance students' learning. The emergence of digital audio tools in classroom environments has created improved learning opportunities for students as well as leveled the playing field for many students who struggle with reading, writing, and language skills. For instance, tools that provide playback read-aloud features of digital stories and allow students to simultaneously read and hear words as they follow along in text supports reading comprehension skills for students who may struggle with decoding and fluency skills. These tools also enhance students' digital literacy skills as they read and navigate digital texts. Additionally, having students create digital audio texts may also aid in the retention and reinforcement of content that may be accessed by multiple users, while developing new literacies such as the use of digital tools to record and broadcast information (Putman & Kingsley, 2009). Yet, students must be given multiple opportunities to practice using digital audio tools, particularly to refine the digital composition skills necessary for recording, editing, and publishing a digital audio file. In this chapter, we discuss multiple user-friendly tools to aid in this process and improve students' use of digital audio tools that may support traditional and new literacies.

COMMON CORE CONNECTIONS

We also consider how the Common Core State Standards (CCSS) address the use of digital audio tools in the classroom. Particularly, the CCSS place a strong emphasis on students' listening and speaking skills, evidenced by the strand of anchor standards devoted to this area of literacy. Digital audio tools can support students' learning and address many of the standards in this strand such as evaluating media (CCSS.ELA-Literacy.CCRA.SL.2), expressing information and ideas through various modes of media (CCSS. ELA-Literacy.CCRA.SL.5), and demonstrating command of formal English (CCSS.ELA-Literacy.CCRA.SL.6). We also describe ways to have students work with others on activities using digital audio, which encourages students to collaboratively build on and express ideas clearly and persuasively (CCSS. ELA-Literacy.CCRA.SL.1). Although many reading-based anchor standards may certainly be addressed with the use of digital audio tools to support reading, we are encouraged by how these tools support all learners in independent reading and comprehension of complex literary and informational texts (CCSS.ELA-Literacy.CCRA.R.10). We believe these connections to the CCSS are relevant for both planning and enriching instruction with digital audio tools, as all of these standards are essential for a well-rounded literacy curriculum.

USING DIGITAL AUDIO TOOLS IN THE CLASSROOM

Audio Recording Students' Reading for Self-evaluation, Teacher Evaluation, or to Share

Digital audio tools can be used to record reading for a variety of purposes. Mobile devices such as iPods, tablets, and smart phones have built-in microphones that make it simple for students to digitally record and share their products. One way that digital audio recordings can be used is for students to record themselves reading a book so that they can listen to it and evaluate their own fluency. Students can also use these recordings to share with other students in the class. One unique way we have seen students share their reading is by posting their recording of their reading to a podcasting site and then generating a quick response (QR) code for the site. Students then printed out the code and taped it to the front of the book they read. Other students in the class could then scan the QR code with the class iPad and listen to their classmate's reading of the story. This activity can be motivating for both the student who produces the recording and the student who gets to listen to it. It also provides the student who is recording their reading with a purpose and audience for reading. QR codes can be easily generated through a QR code generator website. We like https://www.the-qrcode-generator.com. Alternately, there are sites, such as www.chirbit.com that allow the user to record and generate a QR code for sharing all within the same site.

Another way that students can share their reading is by posting it to a class site and then sharing the link through their class Twitter account. Recently in a first grade classroom, we saw students recording themselves using www. chirbit.com. Each week, a different student was the featured reader and that student composed a message to go with the link to the recording and posted it to the class Twitter page (www.twitter.com). The purpose of posting it to Twitter was so that parents could have a link to what was happening in the classroom (students were guided in posting many tweets throughout the day), so that students could gain experience composing meaningful messages through social media, and so that students would have a meaningful audience for which to record their readings.

Another purpose for digitally audio recording students' reading is for teachers to listen to the reading to evaluate students' fluency progress. Specifically, teachers can record students' performance on a running record and use it to conduct a miscue analysis. By recording students at several points throughout the year, teachers can listen to the recordings to make comparisons and gauge students' progress over time. Teachers can also share these recordings with students or with parents during conferences as evidence of progress. Recording students' reading is simple, and, with instruction, even young readers can do it independently during center time when the teacher is working with other students.

Another way we have seen digital audio tools used is to create podcasts of students' Readers Theatre performances. Readers Theatre has been shown to improve fluency and comprehension, likely due to the repeated readings it involves and the authenticity and engagement it brings to the task of reading. Recording students' Readers Theatre performances to share with an audience that extends beyond the classroom can further increase the authenticity of this literacy activity and has been shown to result in comprehension gains (Vasinda & McLeod, 2011).

Sharing Expertise with Podcasts

In addition to creating podcasts of fiction reading performances, students can create informational podcasts related to topics they are studying, particularly in content areas such as science and social studies. Other ideas include creating podcasts of students interviewing community members who use math or science in their jobs, creating a "this day in history" podcast, or podcasting a book review. We have also observed teachers and schools create web pages where students' podcasts are hosted and students from other schools subscribe to the students' feed to discover what they are learning at their school.

One example comes from this fifth grade classroom: http://mrcoley.com/coleycast/index.htm. Students in this class created podcasts on a variety of topics and published them to a class site and to iTunes. If you are interested in learning more about how to begin podcasting in the classroom, we suggest you visit this informational site: http://beyondpenguins.ehe.osu.edu/issue/polar-oceans/podcasts-in-the-elementary-classroom-tools-for-teachers-and-students.

Supporting Out of School Learning

Podcasts can also be used to support learning outside of school. Putman & Kingsley (2009) described how they created podcasts with science-specific vocabulary to provide additional vocabulary instruction for students. They discovered the podcasts to be valuable tools because they afforded students the opportunity to review content outside of class and re-listen to content they had forgotten or that was confusing. The permanency of the podcasts allowed for anytime learning and multiple exposures to the content, yet the podcasts were efficient and were not disruptive to the rhythm of the classroom. Additionally, the ability to add visual prompts to the podcasts was beneficial as students were able to use picture cues to prompt their memory as they reviewed science vocabulary. They also reported that the podcasts were engaging for students because they were able to add music, dramatic effects, and humor to make the science vocabulary more interesting and memorable. Similar podcasts could be created to provide students with background knowledge on a topic they will soon be studying or reading about. This type of podcast could be particularly beneficial for English Learners or other students who may not have the same background knowledge as most students in the class and need extra support.

Using Audio Tools to Respond to Text

Digital audio recording can also be used as a means of responding to text to demonstrate comprehension. Students can also combine audio with images to further support their response. A fourth grade classroom used the Sundry Notes app for iPad to respond to text. The teacher wanted students to understand cause and effect relationships and found that the students were having a difficult time writing about their understanding of cause and effect, so she allowed them to instead respond by drawing illustrations and orally explaining them. The Sundry Notes app allows the user to insert an audio recording into a document. Thus, the students drew illustrations to show cause and effect relationships they had found in a story and then inserted an audio note into the document to explain their illustrations. The students then exported their documents to the teacher directly from the app. The teacher was able to later listen to the audio recordings to determine the extent to which students understood the target concepts. Allowing her students to respond in this way supported them as they learned about these complex textual relationships and acted as a scaffold in their learning.

We also like the use of digital storybook tools to support learning about informational topics that might create connections among literacy and other content areas. Tools such as My Story-Book Maker, which is used in the sample lesson plan at the end of this chapter, may be used for application beyond creating fictional texts and traditional story telling. These types of tools create opportunities for students to extend their learning about writing and narrating of informational texts in social studies and science. Students may summarize and reinforce learning about content area topics with these types of tools, while simultaneously honing speaking and listening skills, along with digital literacy skills in the production of digital texts that include audio and images.

Providing Feedback on Writing

Digital audio tools can be used by both teachers and students to provide feedback on students' writing. This use can be particularly beneficial for teachers who must respond to large amounts of student writing, both digital and non-digital. Rather than writing lengthy responses, teachers can create audio recordings for their students that explain the teacher's reaction to the writing, revisions that need to be made, and the next steps that student needs to take. Students can listen to this recording prior to conferencing with the teacher so that he or she can come to the conference prepared with questions or areas for clarification and the conference time can be spent with the teacher providing the specific support that the student needs rather than just explaining where changes are needed.

Students can also use this type of response to react to their peers' writing or even to respond to published writing such as a book, website, or blog. As with teachers, responding in this way can be helpful for students because they do not have to write lengthy responses and they can fully explain their thinking through their oral explanation. Further, students can read and respond during their independent work time or even outside of school. This frees up class time for students to further discuss their work and take steps toward improving it. We also highlight considerations for teachers to digitally respond to students' work in Textbox 5.1.

Textbox 5.1.

Focus On:
Responding to Students' Digital Work

Challenge: One major challenge of grading students, digital work, unlike paper-based assignments, is that providing feedback can be difficult when the final work product is digital and may be in PDF or JPG format. Teachers want to give specific, detailed feedback about components of the digital product, but they are unable to write extensively on students' work to elaborate their grading decisions. A rubric may be useful, but sometimes you want students to pay particular attention to a certain aspect of the product not addressed specifically in the rubric. Additionally, because teachers may not be accustomed to grading digital work products, assessment may be time consuming.

Consider: Digital work products may not need to be graded in the same format as traditional paper-based products, and students' use of technology should also be considered in assessment to address digital literacy skills.

Tips:
1. Often, digitally-based assignments may be better completed in pairs or small groups, minimizing the amount of grading for each student.
2. Use digital feedback tools, such as Jing, to capture screen and audio feedback in video format that students can play back to review their grade.
3. Provide the product grade at the end of the feedback video so that students watch/listen to all feedback.
4. Email students their feedback or post it on individual student grade boards (if using a digital learning platform) so that students and their parents can access feedback.

Check out: *Jing* (www.jing.com)

Jing is a digital tool to create a share videos of a computer screen with audio. Simply talk your way through a student's digital product opened on your computer screen to point out elements of the product, using the mouse to highlight as you talk. View an online tutorial of Jing here: www.techsmith .com/tutorial-jing.html.

SAMPLE LESSON PLAN

The lesson plan in Table 5.1 uses three digital apps on an iPad to engage students in developing, writing, and narrating an informational text. This lesson plan builds on the use of digital images discussed in chapter 4. If you do not have classroom iPads, digital voice recorders may be used for the

Table 5.1. Sample Third-grade Lesson Using My Story-Book Maker to Create and Narrate an Informational Text

Instructional Goals of the lesson:
- Students will develop and narrate an informational text about herbivores, carnivores, and omnivores (animals) using the My Story-Book Maker app for iPad.
- With a partner, students will brainstorm information by interviewing one another and recording the interview using the Voice Recorder app on iPad.
- Students will listen to recorded interviews to develop an outline using the list feature on the Evernote app on iPad.
- Students will search for images on the Internet or take pictures using the iPad camera to include in their text.

Common Core Standards Addressed:
CCSS.ELA-Literacy.W.3.2
Write informative/explanatory texts to examine a topic and convey ideas and information clearly.
CCSS.ELA-Literacy.W.3.4
With guidance and support from adults, produce writing in which the development and organization are appropriate to task and purpose.
CCSS.ELA-Literacy.SL.3.3
Ask and answer questions about information from a speaker, offering appropriate elaboration and detail.
CCSS.ELA-Literacy.SL.3.4
Report on a topic or text, tell a story, or recount an experience with appropriate facts and relevant, descriptive details, speaking clearly at an understandable pace.
CCSS.ELA-Literacy.L.3.1
Demonstrate command of the conventions of standard English grammar and usage when writing or speaking.
CCSS.ELA-Literacy.L.3.3
Use knowledge of language and its conventions when writing, speaking, reading, or listening.

English Language Proficiency Standards Addressed:
1. Participate in grade-appropriate oral and written exchanges of information, ideas, and analyses, responding to peer, audience, or reader comments and questions
2. Speak and write about grade-appropriate complex literary and informational texts and topics
1. Conduct research and evaluate and communicate findings to answer questions or solve problems
7. Adapt language choices to purpose, task, and audience when speaking and writing
8. Determine the meaning of words and phrases in oral presentations and literary and informational text
9. Create clear and coherent grade-appropriate speech and text
10. Make accurate use of standard English to communicate in grade-appropriate speech and writing

Lesson Description & Instructional Approach:
This lesson will be completed in partners and over multiple classes. Each pair of students will create one informational text.

- After studying herbivores, carnivores, and omnivores in science, students will be paired together to interview one another using teacher-developed questions focusing on traits of the different animal types. One student will serve as the interviewer and the other the interviewee. These interviews will guide students to determine the type of animal they will focus on when developing their informational text, and help students recount information about each type of animal.
- Students will record interviews using the Voice Recorder app on iPad by:
  ° Pressing the record button on the graphic of the cassette recorder.
  ° Stopping the recording at the end of the interview or if the interviewee requests a break.
  ° Labeling the recording with a title of the student's name and date of recording.
  ° Checking the recording for clarity and sound by playing the recording to the interviewee.
- Students will then listen to the interview to determine which type of animal to focus on in their informational text and to consider information to include in the text.
- Students will search for or capture five images they will use to provide illustrations of animals or food sources to support their text narration. They will save these pictures in the iPad camera roll.
- Students will use Evernote to outline their text by:
  ° Using the list feature to create a new bulleted outline.
  ° Importing each of the photos or pictures they saved to the camera roll to the list outline and collaboratively writing the text under each picture that they will use to narrate the text based on their interview responses.
  ° Students will use this outline to create their informational text and to read during narration.
- My Story-Book Maker will be used to develop their text using these steps:
  ° Students will create a book cover and open a new page to begin their text.
  ° They will select the first picture they captured or found from the camera roll using the picture button at the bottom of the screen.
  ° One student will edit the picture on the page, and the other will read and record the text written for that image from their Evernote outline.
  ° Students will repeat this process, switching roles with each page, until all pictures have been included and the text consists of six digital pages, including the title page. This process will develop the students' informational textbook.
- After students have edited and created their books, they will rotate around the room in pairs visiting each iPad to view and listen to their classmates' texts.

See Figures 5.1 and 5.2 for screenshots of an Evernote outline created for this lesson and the first page of the informational text created in My Story-Book Maker. To listen to and view the first page of this story, visit http://msty.me/1o284xR.

Digital Tools/Apps/Websites Used:
- Voice recorder app
- Digital camera/camera roll
- Internet web browser for locating pictures
- Evernote
- My Story-Book Maker for Kids

(continued)

Table 5.1. (*continued*)

Digital Contribution to Instruction:
- Using interviews and the voice recorder students will demonstrate and practice oral language skills and questioning skills while practicing digital skills, such as using digital technology to record and play audio speech.
- Using these tools provides a collaborative way for students to develop, write, and narrate a digital informational text.
- Students practice using digital tools (voice recorder and Evernote) to prepare and outline an informational text.
- Students practice using web browsers to locate images.
- Images saved on camera roll may be used for other instructional activities.
- Students' creation of digital informational texts with narration reinforces comprehension of information and oral language skills.
- Once the book is completed in My Story-Book Maker, it can be imported to iBooks library, so that students can share their texts in a common classroom space.

Potential Constraints:
- Students may struggle with locating pictures online if they do not have practice searching for and locating information through an online search engine. **Solution:** Teachers may modify this step by adding identified images and websites to a secure classroom site, such as Google Plus, to limit students' search parameters on the Internet and help them practice finding images online.
- The uses of multiple digital tools may overwhelm students. **Solution:** This lesson was developed to take place over multiple classes. Focusing on one type of technology per class may simplify the process and mini-lessons with modeling may support students' use of each type of digital tool. Providing students with multiple opportunities to practice using technology in this and in other class activities will also streamline this lesson.
- Students may struggle with writing a narrative for an informational text. **Solution:** Provide students with examples of narratives or model an outline, with guiding prompts, for students to follow as they write the narrative that they will record.

Instructional Considerations:
- Evernote requires users to sign in with an e-mail address and password. The teacher can decide whether students will use their school-provided email addresses or if they will use a teacher-designated email address.
- My Story-Book Maker is not a free app, so teachers with iPad access may inquire about purchasing this app.

Reflection:
After the lesson is complete, consider the literacy skills you saw promoted by this lesson. How might you modify the lesson in the future to make stronger connections between literacy learning in this lesson and in other classroom activities? Was collaboration a positive aspect of this lesson, or did students struggle working with partners? What modifications to technology may be useful in this lesson?

Figure 5.1.   Screenshot of outline created in Evernote.

interviewing portion of the lesson, and the apps may be installed on computers to follow the same lesson plan. We selected the digital tool, My Story-Book Maker (http://mystoryapp.org), for this lesson because it allows students to create stories using images, audio, and written text. A tutorial for My Story-Book maker may be found at http://youtu.be/Ixq1GncoZ6I, although we also

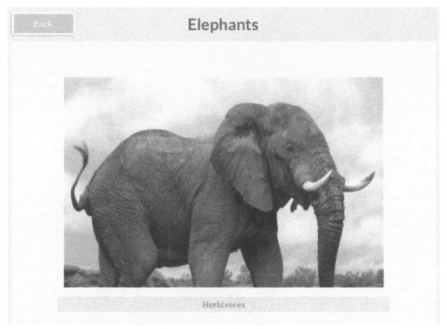

Figure 5.2.   Screenshot of the first page of the informational textbook on elephants as herbivores.

encourage teachers to allow students time to play with the app to become familiar with its features. This lesson plan was developed for grade three, but could be adapted for kindergarten through sixth grade.

RESOURCES

As in previous chapters, we provide here a table of resources for using digital audio technology in instruction. We hope you will explore the various tools and apps listed in this table to consider how you might use them to promote literacy skills in your K-6 classroom.

REFLECTION QUESTIONS

1. Digital audio tools are simple to use and can support students' learning in many ways. What are some of the ways that you and your students can use digital audio tools to help students meet their literacy goals?

Table 5.2. Resources and Sample Activities for Integrating Digital Audio Tools

Digital Resources	Possible Uses	Grade-Specific Examples & CCSS Addressed
Digital Tools: • Audio recorder • iPod	Students may: • Record oral readings of stories • Conduct interviews • Practice reading aloud various texts Teachers may: • Record students' reading of texts to create running records or provide feedback to students and parents. • Record class activities to support student reflection about learning and their performance during activities.	With a family member, first grade students could orally retell an important life event (e.g., birthday, getting a new pet) and record it using an audio recorder. The teacher could post these stories to a class webpage or wiki to create an important events in my life page. **CCSS.ELA-Literacy.W.1.6.** *With guidance and support from adults, use a variety of digital tools to produce and publish writing, including in collaboration with peers.* **CCSS.ELA-Literacy.W.1.8.** *With guidance and support from adults, recall information from experiences or gather information from provided sources to answer a question.* A sixth-grade student may interview a World War II veteran, record the interview, and then summarize the interview with links to the recording on their school blog page. **CCSS.ELA-Literacy.SL.6.4.** *Present claims and findings, sequencing ideas logically and using pertinent descriptions, facts, and details to accentuate main ideas or themes; use appropriate eye contact, adequate volume, and clear pronunciation.* **CCSS.ELA-Literacy.SL.6.1.** *Engage effectively in a range of collaborative discussions (one-on-one, in groups, and teacher-led) with diverse partners on grade 6 topics, texts, and issues, building on others' ideas and expressing their own ideas clearly.*

(continued)

Table 5.2. (continued)

Digital Resources	Possible Uses	Grade-Specific Examples & CCSS Addressed
Apps: • Chirbit • Good Reader • My Story Book Maker • Sundry Notes • SoundNote • Voice Recorder • AudioNote • Super Note • Recordium	Students may: • Develop and record oral retellings of stories • Draw and orally explain different aspects of a literary text • Annotate texts orally to take notes • Listen to texts while reading along Teachers may: • Listen to students' oral note-taking and provide oral feedback. • Develop classroom informational texts to provide texts for students to use independently to further study a topic.	With assistance from a teacher, a kindergarten student could digitally paint or draw a picture and orally explain and record the events occurring in the picture. **CCSS.ELA-Literacy.W.K.2.** *Use a combination of drawing, dictating, and writing to compose informative/explanatory texts in which they name what they are writing about and supply some information about the topic.* Third grade students could highlight sections of a digital poem and create voice annotations to denote important literary elements. **CCSS.ELA-Literacy.RL.5.4.** *Determine the meaning of words and phrases as they are used in a text, including figurative language such as metaphors and similes.*
Online Resources: • Audioboo • Jing • Podbean • VoiceThread • Voxopop	Students may: • Create podcasts of book reviews and reactions to text • Create instructional podcasts • Host a podcast on fiction or nonfiction texts or life events • Improve listening and speaking skills on an audio message board • Report on various topics for a classroom news segment or school news and broadcast the show Teachers may: • Provide oral feedback to students on digital projects, papers, and activities. • Create a podcast for parents with classroom and school news.	Third-grade students may read or listen to retellings of Native American oral narratives, and then create, record, and broadcast their own oral narrative in the same tradition using a podcast. **CCSS.ELA-Literacy.RL.3.2.** *Recount stories, including fables, folktales, and myths from diverse cultures; determine the central message, lesson, or moral and explain how it is conveyed through key details in the text.* After studying a unit on journalism and ethical reporting, a fourth-grade classroom could create their own news show and either broadcast the show as a podcast, or invite guests to interview on a hosted podcast. **CCSS.ELA-Literacy.SL.4.4.** *Report on a topic or text, tell a story, or recount an experience in an organized manner, using appropriate facts and relevant, descriptive details to support main ideas or themes; speak clearly at an understandable pace.*

2. Do your students have good listening skills? Consider how you can use podcasts produced by other classes to help your students develop listening skills and learn about new topics. Consider partnering with a class in another school, state, or country to establish an authentic audience for podcasts that students create.

REFERENCES

International Reading Association & National Association for the Education of Young Children. (1998). *Learning to read and write: Developmentally appropriate practices for young children.* Newark, DE; Washington, DC: Authors.

Kress, G. (2003). *Literacy in the new media age.* New York, NY: Routledge.

Putman, S., & Kingsley, T. (2009). The Atoms Family: Using Podcasts to Enhance the Development of Science Vocabulary. *The Reading Teacher, 63*(2), 100–8. doi:10.1598/RT.63.2.1

Snow, C. E., Burns, M. S., & Griffin, P. (Eds.). (1998). *Preventing reading difficulties in young children.* Washington, DC: National Academy Press.

Vasinda, S., & McLeod, J. (2011). Extending readers theatre: A powerful and purposeful match with podcasting. *The Reading Teacher, 64*(7), 486–97. doi:10.1598/RT.64.7.2

Chapter Six

Using Digital Graphic Organizer Tools in the Classroom

The students in Mrs. Johnson's class are rapidly developing their digital and non-digital literacy skills. Because they are enjoying their literacy activities and instruction so much, they are eager to continue learning. She will continue to help her students develop their reading comprehension skills and digital literacy skills as she introduces digital graphic organizers to them this month. Her students will use digital graphic organizers to support their learning in many ways, such as creating summaries and retellings, learning new vocabulary words, and organizing their writing. Meanwhile, her students will continue to use their previously developed skills by incorporating images and audio recordings into their organizers. The lesson in Table 6.1 shows how Mrs. Johnson had her students combine images and text in a graphic organizer to develop their understanding of a social studies topic. Despite students' increasing digital skills, as she plans her lesson, Mrs. Johnson recognizes that her students may still need support in learning how to use the graphic organizer tool she has selected. Therefore, she plans a short minilesson on how to use the tool. Additionally, she has to figure out how students can save their work, since unlike other digital tools her students have used, Popplet lite does not require students to sign into an account. However, after some creative thinking, she is able to overcome these potential constraints and integrate these tools into her classroom.

A key ingredient in fostering and structuring reading and writing to improve comprehension is helping students organize their thoughts and ideas. Often, when we think of the term graphic organizers we think of a tool to outline a text students are preparing to write or to organize the main ideas and supporting details of a text they are reading. We also often think of worksheets with concept maps or diagrams ready to be completed. Yet, graphic organizers may be used for much more than preparing to read or guiding reading, and the digital revolution has changed the way in which we use and prepare graphic organizers. Particularly at the elementary grade levels, digital graphic organizer tools offer ways for students to represent their thoughts or ideas using different fonts, colors, images, and even audio to consider what a text means or to write their own text. The graphic organizer may become, essentially, a text in and of itself. The question to consider in this chapter, then is, "how might I incorporate graphic organizers into my classroom in meaningful ways to promote both reading and writing?"

As you will read in this chapter, numerous digital graphic organizer tools exist to assist students and to make seamless connections between digital and traditional literacy skills. We urge you to consider how you may use digital graphic organizer tools to prepare students to learn, to guide them, and to help them reflect on their learning. Certainly, different grade levels will need various levels of support, but the beauty of digital graphic organizer tools is they can be used by students who are learning to read and write and those that are reading and writing to learn, spanning the spectrum of K-6 literacy learning.

COMMON CORE CONNECTIONS

As we have noted with other digital tools in previous chapters, the Common Core State Standards also promote anchor learning objectives that may be easily and readily targeted through the incorporation of digital graphic organizer tools. As students read closely to comprehend or analyze narrative text (CCSS.ELA-Literacy.CCRA.R.1) graphic organizer tools may help map out and capture students' thinking so that they may revisit text and ideas while they are reading. As upper elementary students begin to analyze structures of text and how various textual elements (i.e., chapters and stanzas) relate to one another (CCSS.ELA-Literacy.CCRA.R.5), digital graphic organizers may be used to chart this analysis. When students are asked to orally tell or write texts, graphic organizer tools may also be used to structure and outline their narratives to convey complex ideas clearly (CCSS.ELA-Literacy. CCRA.W.2). Digital graphic organizers will also be useful in the production of clear writing that attends to development, organization, and style appropriate to task, purpose, and audience (CCSS.ELA-Literacy.CCRA.W.4). Finally, if using graphic organizers as a product of student thinking to represent an idea or knowledge gained, students can both integrate and evaluate information using diverse formats (CCSS.ELA-Literacy.CCRA.SL.2) and make strategic use of digital media and visual displays to express information (CCSS.ELA-Literacy.CCRA.SL.5). The remainder of this chapter outlines more specific methods to use digital graphic organizers, types of tools useful for creating graphic organizers, and a detailed lesson plan to incorporate graphic organizer tools into your classroom.

DIGITAL GRAPHIC ORGANIZERS IN THE CLASSROOM

Creating Summaries and Retellings

Because most graphic organizer tools have many functions and options, they allow the user to determine the purpose and format of what is created with the tool. Tools such as the iBrainstorm app allow the user to determine how notes are organized, assign colors to give additional meaning or priority, to draw, write or type text, and to collaboratively work on a document shared to different devices. With this tool, students could collaborate to create a visual retelling. Conducting a retelling with a graphic organizer tool, such as iBrainstorm, can provide a way for students to organize their thoughts and ensure that they have included pertinent details (see Figure 6.1 for a screenshot of a iBrainstorm organizer). Additionally, by using a tool that allows multiple users to contribute and collaborate, students will potentially be able

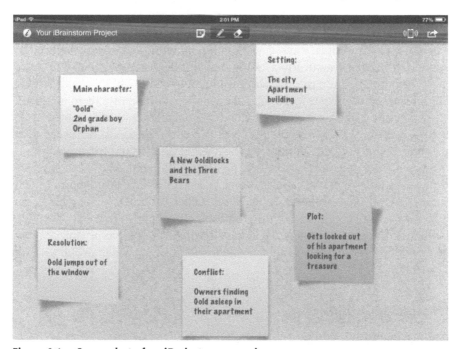

Figure 6.1. Screenshot of an iBrainstorm organizer.

to construct a more thorough retelling by sharing their ideas and checking each other's work.

Reading Comprehension Strategies

Graphic organizer tools can also be used to provide practice on many different reading comprehension strategies such as identifying main ideas and details, sequencing events, creating timelines, distinguishing fact and opinion, identifying problems and solutions, and determining cause and effect relationships in a text. Although there are many graphic organizer apps that allow students to create their own structure, there are also apps that come pre-loaded with graphic organizer tools aimed at guiding students in practicing reading comprehension strategies. For example, the Tools 4 Students app comes with twenty-five different graphic organizers such as KWL charts, anticipation guides, characterization charts and more. These pre-structured organizers may be more beneficial for younger students or for students who are not yet ready to create their own organizational structure. One benefit of creating these organizers digitally rather than using pencil and paper is that they can easily be saved for later reference and can be shared digitally.

Vocabulary Learning

There are also multiple ways that digital graphic organizers can be used to support vocabulary acquisition. Using digital tools has the potential to make these activities more engaging and meaningful by allowing students to add photos and other images to go with the words. Additionally, there are many apps that allow the user to create playful organizers with different shapes, colors, and fonts. One example of a tool that could be useful for vocabulary learning is the Perfect Captions app. This app allows the user to add multiple captions to pictures. Therefore, this app could be used to have students capture an image of a vocabulary term and use the caption function to add examples and non-examples of the term. Other examples of graphic organizers that can be created with digital tools to support vocabulary learning include Vocab-O-Grams and Semantic Webs. Also, graphic organizers may be beneficial for English Language Learners (ELLs), which we discuss in Textbox 6.1.

Organizing Writing

Among the most obvious uses of digital graphic organizer tools is organizing writing. There are an abundance of apps that help writers do everything

Textbox 6.1.

Focus On:

Using Digital Mind Mapping to support English Language Learners (ELLs)

Challenge: Vocabulary-based academic activities can be daunting for ELLs who struggle with reading, speaking, and writing the English language. ELLs must often memorize or learn lists of words that they are unfamiliar with but are critical to learning content. Further, academic vocabulary usually differs from informal vocabulary used in everyday out-of-school language, making it more difficult to learn than the frequently used English vocabulary.

Consider: Mind maps are non-linear outlines used to help students "map out" ideas using a graphic organizer, phrases, or images to better understand a topic, to help students learn vocabulary.

Tips:
1. Create small groups consisting of native speakers and ELLs to have students map out focal vocabulary using a graphic organizer, while supporting one another in learning.
2. Decide whether you will have your students use a digital mind-mapping tool that already provides a structured format or if you will allow students to structure their own mind-map. Pre-structured organizers may ensure that students learn specific information, while build-your-own organizers allow students freedom of thought in making connections.
3. Have students orally discuss their reasoning for connections in their small groups to collaboratively build mind maps focused on academic vocabulary.
4. Visit each small group to informally assess progress and provide oral feedback to build students' oral language skill.
5. Encourage students to use images and text in their mind maps, and print out and hang final mind maps on the wall to support continued vocabulary learning. You may also wish to share the mind maps through social media or post them to a section of a class blog or website that is focused on academic vocabulary.

Check Out: *SpiderScribe* (www.spiderscribe.net) See Figure 6.2 for a screenshot of a simple mind map describing weather vocabulary.

SpiderScribe offers a free mind-mapping tool that students can use to build mind maps that they can build and share with one another in a public space.

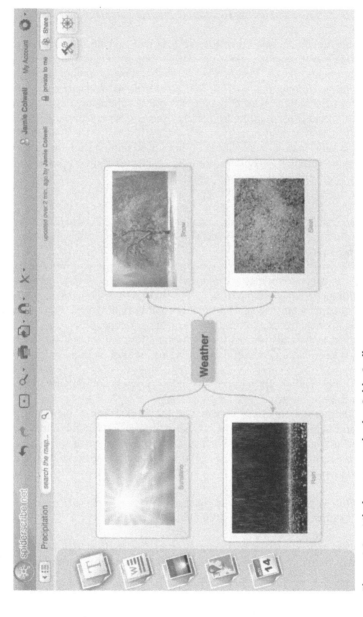

Figure 6.2. Mindmap created using SpiderScribe.

from creating an outline to organizing multiple pieces of writing into digital notebooks. One use of organizer tools that can be helpful for students is for collecting ideas for writing. This use may be particularly valuable for writing informative or explanatory texts. Tools such as Evernote allow students to collect web pages, files, notes, photos, and videos into a single "notebook" that they create. Multiple notebooks can be created to organize information on different topics. Evernote can be used on both computers and tablets and an account can be accessed from anywhere, not just within an app on a particular device, so students can continue to work outside of class. Basic graphic organizer tools, such as Popplet, are also helpful for organizing writing because they allow the user to insert images and drawings along with text. This approach can be useful for organizing writing that will be accompanied by images, such as presentations, movies, and blog and website posts. Websites such as www.creately.com are also helpful because they provide examples and libraries of a wide variety of graphic organizers.

SAMPLE LESSON PLAN

The lesson plan presented in Table 6.1 uses digital graphic organizers to present information as a culmination of learning in social studies. By using graphic organizers for purposes of this lesson, students will connect ELA and

Table 6.1. Third Grade Lesson Plan on Using Digital Graphic Organizers to Support Vocabulary Development

Instructional Goals of the lesson:
Students will reflect on the economic terms *producers* and *consumers* using digital graphic organizers to organize and present information.

Common Core Standards Addressed:
CCSS.ELA-LITERACY.RI.3.2
Determine the main idea of a text; recount the key details and explain how they support the main idea.
CCSS.ELA-Literacy.W.3.2
Write informative/explanatory texts to examine a topic and convey ideas and information clearly.
Note: The sub-standards for W.3.2 also apply to this lesson.
CCSS.ELA-Literacy.W.3.6
With guidance and support from adults, use technology to produce and publish writing (using keyboarding skills) as well as to interact and collaborate with others.
CCSS.ELA-Literacy.L.3.3
Use knowledge of language and its conventions when writing, speaking, reading, or listening.

(*continued*)

Table 6.1. (*continued*)

English Language Proficiency Standards Addressed:
1. Construct meaning from oral presentations and literary and informational text through grade-appropriate listening, reading, and viewing.
2. Participate in grade-appropriate oral and written exchanges of information, ideas, and analyses, responding to peer, audience, or reader comments and questions.
3. Speak and write about grade-appropriate complex literary and informational texts and topics.
4. Construct grade-appropriate oral and written claims and support them with reasoning and evidence.
7. Adapt language choices to purpose, task, and audience when speaking and writing.

Lesson Description & Instructional Approach:
- After studying producers and consumers in social studies, students will be placed into small groups of four to create two digital graphic organizers, in a spider web layout, that represent the information learned using written text and images.
- Each small group will be given two iPads with the Popplet Lite app loaded onto the devices.
- Two students in the small group will share an iPad to create a digital graphic organizer about consumers, and the other two students in the group will use their iPad to create a digital graphic organizer about producers.
- **Each graphic organizer should include:** (1) at least four important ideas about the topic; (2) An image related to each topic; (3) Evidence/a quote from the text to support the idea; (4) an evidence-based opinion about the topic (students should provide reasons for their opinion); and (5) a concluding statement on the page to summarize their ideas about the topic.
- In each pair, students will open the Popplet Lite app and select an image to represent their topic, which will serve as the central bubble in the spider web.
- Students will then create supporting bubbles to connect to the central bubble to explain key characteristics of consumers or producers through written text, display images that provide examples for the characteristics, and explain the importance of both in society. (If necessary, the teacher may have students use notes or text to help them remember information.) To do so, students may:
  ○ Search for and locate images on the web. (Teachers may also provide a cache of pre-selected images on a Google Plus class site.)
  ○ Save images to their iPad to import into the Popplet Lite app.
  ○ Draw images within Popplet Lite.
- Students will use various fonts, colors, spatial techniques to best represent their knowledge of the topic.
- Once students have finished their spider web graphic organizer, they will swap iPads with the other dyad in their small group.
- The teacher will provide students with a teacher-created list of questions to ask one another about their graphic organizer to guide students in critique and revision and to ensure students have met all objectives of learning for this topic in social studies.
- After students have conferenced and revised their graphic organizers, they will take a screenshot of their organizer by holding down the sleep/wake button on top of the iPad and then pressing the home button.

- The teacher will then assist students in e-mailing the image so that the teacher can display the images an interactive whiteboard or share them to a class blog or other social media site.

See Figure 6.3 for a screenshot of a Popplet Lite graphic organizer created for this lesson.

Digital Tools Used:
- iPad
- Popplet app
- Screenshot function
- Email

Digital Contribution to Instruction:
- These tools provide a way for students to collaborate, write and present, in a non-traditional manner, texts that represent student knowledge.
- This lesson connects social studies and ELA literacy skills by having students create digital graphic organizers to show information learned in economics.
- Students practice using web browsers to locate images.
- By having students conference about their developed graphic organizers and engage in subsequent revision, students are engaged in oral language, questioning, and revision activities.
- Images saved on the camera roll may be used for review and for models for future activities.
- Having students draw images using Popplet will develop drawing and representation skills.

Potential Constraints:
- Depending on students' familiarity with Popplet Lite and iPads, this lesson may require mini-lessons to prepare students to use these tools. **Solution:** Teachers may find YouTube tutorial videos useful for preparation (search "Popplet Lite app tutorial" in YouTube (www.youtube.com) for multiple tutorials to consider).
- Students may need more guided assistance with peer revision techniques, depending on the focus of peer-revision in a teacher's curriculum. **Solution:** Mini-lessons or practice during ELA instruction may provide a useful crossover and interdisciplinary instruction between social studies and language arts literacy skills.
- Popplet Lite does not have a save or export function. **Solution:** As the lesson plan suggests, having students take a screenshot of the graphic organizer and later printing the organizers may provide opportunities for students to add bubbles to their organizers after the lesson is complete.

Instructional Considerations:
- As Popplet Lite does not have a save feature, students must complete their graphic organizer in one class period.
- This lesson assumes students have already learned about producers and consumers. Teachers have the option of selecting the amount of resources students may use when developing their graphic organizers.

(continued)

Table 6.1.   (*continued*)

Reflection:
How might you adapt this lesson to have students learn about producers and consumers rather than reflect? What connections can you make between the literacy skills promoted through the use of the digital tools and traditional literacy skills students would typically use when reflecting on this topic? How does the knowledge students presented using a digital graphic organizer in this lesson compare with other traditional writing assignments (e.g., a report or diorama) where students are asked to present information learned?

social studies learning to promote interdisciplinary literacy. We selected the free iPad app Popplet Lite (also available for computers; visit www.popplet. com to learn more about this app) for students to build and develop a digital graphic organizer that can incorporate text and images. A paid version of this app also exists with more features, but the free version of the app provides ample learning opportunities for students. We developed this lesson plan for a third-grade classroom, but it could easily be adapted for lower or higher elementary grades through variations in teacher support, complexity of topic, and requirements for text and images represented.

Table 6.2 provides a listing of resources for using digital graphic organizers in the classroom. The listing of apps and websites is far from exhaustive.

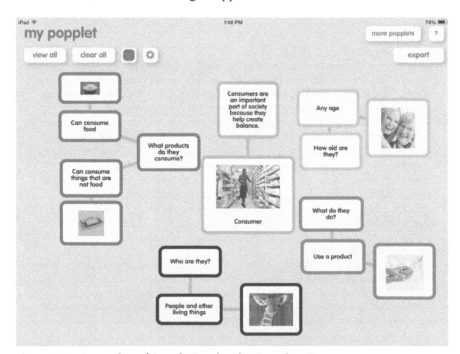

Figure 6.3.   Screenshot of Sample Popplet Lite Organizer Resources

Table 6.2. Resources for Using Digital Graphic Organizer Tools to Support Learning

Digital Resources	Possible Uses	Grade-Specific Examples & CCSS Addressed
Apps: • Popplet • Mindmash • Perfect Captions • Idea Sketch • iBrainstorm • iCard Sort • Inspiration Maps • MindNode • Whiteboard HD • Index Card • Infinote Pinboard • Evernote • Mindly • Pearltrees • Strip Designer • Venn Diagram Online Resources: • www.popplet.com • www.evernote.com • www.pearltrees.com • www.bubbl.us • www.creately.com • www.mindomo.com	Students May: • Create summaries and retellings • Create diagrams of cause and effect relationships • Brainstorm information • Collect related information on a topic • Create timelines • Create charts representing the main ideas of a text and providing supporting details • Create diagrams of vocabulary terms • Create outlines for writing • Share charts and diagrams • Embed diagrams and timelines into a blog or website	**Kindergarten:** With prompting and support from an adult, students may use the Strip Designer app to illustrate the beginning, middle and end of a story. Illustrations should include key details from the story. **CCSS.ELA-LITERACY.RL.K.2** *With prompting and support, retell familiar stories, including key details.* **First Grade:** Students may use the Venn Diagram app to compare information about a science topic found in a picture book and found online (selected by the teacher). **CCSS.ELA-LITERACY.RI.1.9** *Identify basic similarities in and differences between two texts on the same topic (e.g., in illustrations, descriptions, or procedures).* **Second Grade:** Students may use Popplet to create webs for adjectives that the teacher would like for students to incorporate into their writing (such as stupendous or exhilarating). Students place the word in center of the web and then insert images that could be described by the word into boxes around the center of the web. For example, images around stupendous may be of a favorite food, a test receiving an A plus, etc.

(continued)

Table 6.2. (continued)

Digital Resources	Possible Uses	Grade-Specific Examples & CCSS Addressed
• www.mindmeister.com • www.wisemapping.com • www.simplediagrams.com • www.timetoast.com • www.ourstory.com		**CCSS.ELA-LITERACY.L.2.5.A** *Identify real-life connections between words and their use (e.g., describe foods that are spicy or juicy).* **Third Grade:** Students may use the Perfect Captions app to capture an image related to a math term and then insert words that describe the meaning and use of the term by using the caption labels provided in the app. **CCSS.ELA-LITERACY.L.3.6** Acquire and use accurately grade-appropriate conversational, general academic, and domain-specific words and phrases, including those that signal spatial and temporal relationships (e.g., *After dinner that night we went looking for them*). **Fourth Grade:** Students may use wisemapping.com to create a web to illustrate and present the main idea of a science text and the key details that support the idea. **CCSS.ELA-LITERACY.SL.4.5** *Add audio recordings and visual displays to presentations when appropriate to enhance the development of main ideas or themes.*

Fifth Grade: Students may use the T-Chart app to chart the pros and cons related to a science topic and use the chart to an opinion piece on the topic.

CCSS.ELA-LITERACY.W.5.1

Write opinion pieces on topics or texts, supporting a point of view with reasons and information.

Sixth Grade: Use Evernote to create a plant and animal cell notebook in which they label drawings of plant and animal cells and use domain-specific vocabulary to write and explanation of their drawing.

CCSS.ELA-LITERACY.W.5.2.D

Use precise language and domain-specific vocabulary to inform about or explain the topic.

However, we believe that these resources are among those that are easiest to use and potentially most helpful in K-6 classrooms. We hope you will explore the various tools and apps listed in this table to consider how you might use them to promote literacy skills in your K-6 classroom.

REFLECTION QUESTIONS

1. How can graphic organizer tools support students' learning? How can digital graphic organizers further enhance students' work through the features these tools incorporate (such as ability to add images, share digitally, etc.)?
2. Take some time to explore the digital graphic organizer tools listed in Table 6.2. How can you use these tools in the classroom in ways that you might not typically use graphic organizers? For what purposes might you incorporate digital images into the graphic organizers?

Chapter Seven

Digital Writing

Although Mrs. Johnson's students have been using digital tools to write select types of text, Mrs. Johnson wants to introduce them to a wider variety of writing options and wants to show her students the many ways that digital tools can support their writing. Therefore, this month she will focus on helping her students use digital tools for activities such as writing fanfiction and poetry, creating collaborative writing, and creating books that incorporate images and audio recording. Table 7.1 provides an example of how her students will be using TitanPad, a collaborative writing tool, to collaboratively write a fictional story. She chose this tool because she was having difficulty getting the computer lab or iPad cart reserved on a regular basis. Her students have to use different digital devices every day. Since TitanPad will allow her students to save their work online, students can access their work no matter what device they use.

Just as ways of reading have expanded with the increasing prevalence of digital technology, so have ways of writing. Students' writing is no longer limited to sentences, paragraphs, and essays composed with pencil and paper. Rather, with digital technology, students compose writing in a variety of digital formats, such as wiki posts, blog posts, podcast scripts, social media posts, and even their own digital books. With these new formats come new purposes for writing, as well as new audiences. A benefit of digital technology is the ease with which students can share their writing with audiences outside of the classroom. Because of the simplicity of sharing digital writing, students can create writing for many different purposes, which may include everything from sharing information with students in another country to sharing what they did at school that day with their parents. As part of this increased access to outside audiences and an increasing number of digital platforms for writing, students must also learn how to choose the right format or tool for the intended purpose. This knowledge should be a consideration for all teachers as they integrate digital writing into their classrooms. Whatever you choose to take away from this chapter, be certain that your instruction involves the purposes for which students might choose a particular digital tool or platform for composing and communicating a message.

Another benefit of digital technology for writing is the increased opportunity for collaboration and shared writing. Digital platforms such as wikis create a space where students can collect their knowledge and each become contributors to a larger body of knowledge. Tools such as Google Docs make it possible for students to co-author a document in real time without having to physically be in the same space. Other digital platforms, such as blogs, provide a space for students to comment on each other's writing and to share insights. By collaborating and sharing writing projects, students can generate more knowledge and ideas than they would be able to otherwise. Teachers can take advantage of digital tools to increase students' interactions, understandings, and productivity.

COMMON CORE CONNECTIONS

The Common Core State Standards specifically call for students to write with digital tools. For example, one of the anchor standards for writing states that students should "Use technology, including the Internet, to produce and publish writing and to interact and collaborate with others" (CCSS. ELA-LITERACY.CCRA.W.6). Another standard states that students should "Gather relevant information from multiple print and digital sources, assess the credibility and accuracy of each source, and integrate the information while avoiding plagiarism" (CCSS.ELA-LITERACY.CCRA.W.8). In this chapter we will describe some of the ways that digital tools can be integrated into the classroom to provide new audiences, purposes, and formats for writing while also meeting the goals of the Common Core State Standards. We preface this discussion by noting that the previous chapters have discussed digital tools that build up to and may be used in conjunction with writing tools we talk about here. As the chapters in this book gradually incorporate reading, writing, and communicating with digital tools using more advanced literacy skills, you may see an overlap in the use of digital tools and similar digital tools appearing in multiple chapters, although they may be used in different ways.

DIGITAL TOOLS FOR WRITING IN THE CLASSROOM

Writing among Beginning and Struggling Readers and Writers

Although writing using digital tools is usually thought of as a higher-level practice, multiple digital apps for tablets are available to enhance beginning and struggling writers' learning experiences. Many apps that promote writing skills at the beginners' level are geared toward game-playing, which may be motivating for students to practice writing letters and forming sentences. For example, students who are learning to write letters may benefit from apps that allow them to trace letters to practice basic motor skills associated with writing. The iWrite Words app is a low-cost tablet application that helps students hone handwriting skills through a series of games. As students progress and begin to write full words and create sentences, games such as Sentence Builder, that targets grammar and sentence structuring skills may become useful for students to practice writing.

Students who are learning to write or who have cognitive and motor delays in using traditional writing tools such as a pencil may find digital tools that transfer audio dictation to writing to be useful in seeing how words are spelled and look in paragraph form. A common practice in kindergarten and first-grade classrooms is for students to orally tell a story to a teacher or adult to practice narrative skills, which precede but help build literacy skills associated with learning to write. A digital dictation tool, such as Dragon Dictation, allows students to orally tell their narrative to an iPad, tablet, or computer with a microphone and the program transfers the audio feed to writing instantaneously. Students can watch as their oral words become written words. Not only does this practice allow more students to participate in narrative storytelling at one time, if multiple iPads or computers are available, but it also allows students independence in writing at an earlier age. However, teachers must develop supervision systems to monitor and scaffold activities where students dictate their writing, and supplemental follow-up activities are necessary to help students reflect on what they learned using the digital tools.

Brainstorming

As students hone their writing skills throughout early elementary grades and begin to engage in independent or collaborative peer-writing with other classmates, digital tools are available that structure brainstorming activities. In the lesson plan at the end of this chapter, we will discuss how teachers may incorporate digital graphic organizers into their instruction. Such organizers allow students to create mind maps and annotate those maps with notes, images, and audio, which aids in structuring and outlining written texts. Some websites offer free mind map tools that provide basic graphic organizers for students to build and customize to structure their ideas. One such site, bubbl. us (https://bubbl.us), allows students to create up to three free mind maps and save those maps. Figure 7.1 provides a screenshot of an outline developed to structure an informational piece of writing on amphibians.

Although this type of graphic organizer can be completed with pencil and paper, we consider the editing functions of the tool to be useful in helping students organize and reorganize writing in multiple ways using various colors and font sizes to highlight ideas and supporting ideas. Students can easily manipulate the appearance of the bubbles and delete and create new bubbles more efficiently than could be done using pencil and paper.

Teachers may also use digital tools prior to outlining written texts to help students create and formulate ideas for writing. We particularly like the free computer program, Wordle (www.wordle.net) to help students brainstorm ideas to focus their writing. Teachers can have students engage in a timed free write in a Word document on a particular topic to brainstorm their prior knowledge. Students can then copy and paste their free writes into Wordle to create a word cloud of ideas, which will emphasize repetitive words to show big ideas in writing. Teachers and students can use these word clouds to consider information that should be focused on or based on prior knowledge.

Fiction and Poetry Writing

After brainstorming ideas about writing, teachers may also use digital tools to engage students in constructing multiple types of writing in English language arts. From a creative writing perspective, many digital tools offer a host of templates, images, and audio features to help students create their own stories and to assist teachers in integrating fiction story writing into their instruction. For example, lower-grades elementary teachers may use the Story Patch tablet app to aid young students in writing fiction narratives. This type of app allows students to select from different images and page layouts to write a story. Yet, upper-grades elementary teachers may choose to use a more advanced storytelling tool, such as Storybird (www.storybird.com), that allows students with more advanced writing skills to develop paragraph-long texts that incorporate images to support the texts.

Poetry writing is often an area of writing that many students struggle with as it requires knowledge about poetry structure and advanced thinking about descriptive language. However, digital tools may help scaffold students' writing and thinking about forming poetry. Scholastic offers a free website,

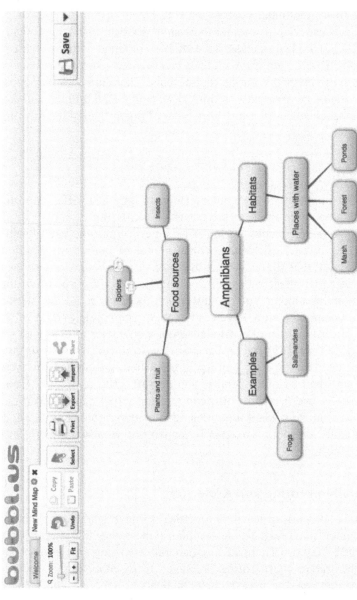

Figure 7.1. Screenshot of mind map created with bubbl.us

Poetry Engine (http://teacher.scholastic.com/writewit/poetry/poetry_engine.
htm), that allows students to consider different types of poetry, such as a
haiku or limerick, with quick and animated tutorials and then engage in writing using fill-in-the-blank poetry games to create different types of poems.
Teachers can use such a website to prompt students' thinking about a type
of poetry being studied in class, have students practice with pre-made poems
on the website, and then have students create their own poems from scratch
using the skills learned with the digital tools. There are also free apps from
ReadWriteThink (www.readwritethink.org), called Haiku Poem and Acrostic
Poem, that teach students about these types of poems and guide them in writing their own.

Fanfiction

Teachers of upper-grade elementary students may also offer opportunities
for students to hone their creative writing skills out-of-school or during
free reading/writing blocks during class time through the use of fanfiction
websites (see www.fanfiction.net for examples of fanfiction). Fanfiction is
a type of fiction that allows writers to create stories, books, or movies based
on characters that already exist in works of fiction. This type of writing has
become popular among young adolescents because it allows students to
write about characters they have read about or seen on television or in film.
Students can use existing knowledge about a character to create an entirely
new storyline for that character based on the students' interests or goals for
the character. This type of writing is published and shared on fanfiction
websites and read by other people who read or write fanfiction. Fanfiction
writers usually use usernames instead of their actual names when publishing their writing, so student identities remain anonymous. Fanfiction can be
found on many sites, but www.fanfiction.net is currently the world's largest
archive of fanfiction.

Collaborative Writing and Reflection

Digital tools also afford teachers a method to have students collaboratively
write documents and text. The lesson plan at the end of this chapter describes
how teachers may use Titanpad, a collaborative writing site, to have students
write collaborative short stories. However, many other digital tools hosted
on the Internet may be used to have students collaborate and post writing
to respond to other students' or the teacher's writing in a reflective manner.
For instance, teachers may use a class blog site using Blogger (www.blogger
.com) to post writing prompts for students to respond to online. This type of

activity may span content areas and allow teachers to integrate ELA into history and science content areas.

An activity that we consider beneficial for using a blog site with writing prompts for reflection and collaboration is for a teacher to post a prompt to gather students' reactions about a lesson. Students can then post responses to the prompt as an exit slip. This process allows teachers to gather assessment data and allows students to read other classmates' reactions to a lesson to further their understanding or consideration of a topic. The teacher can then post responses to students' posts, engaging students in collaborative writing and providing one-on-one attention to each students' understandings of a lesson. We discuss this process further in Table 7.1. Some blog sites, such as Edmodo (www.edmodo.com), allow students to also send responses directly to a teacher so that other students cannot see their responses. This type of exit slip may be appealing if teachers were to prompt students to write about confusing aspects of a lesson. Teachers may also have students create their own blog sites to post reflections to reading and class work, which would serve as a space in which students have unlimited access to engage in writing. Teachers may allow students to choose to make their blog sites public to other classmates, which could also support students in reacting to writing and engaging in collaboration using digital tools. We like blog sites Kidblog (www .kidblog.org) and Edublog (www.edublogs.org) for creating student blogs.

A micro-blog is another possible tool to incite reflection and encourage collaboration in writing. Recently, the use of Twitter (www.twitter.com) has found its way into classrooms. Twitter is a micro-blog that only allows users to post writing of 140 characters or less. Although people often associate Twitter with mainstream popular culture news, Barone and Mallette (2013) share multiple possibilities for using Twitter in the elementary classroom.

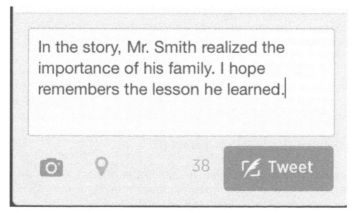

Figure 7.2.   Using Twitter to tweet ideas about a story.

Students may create collaborative short stories via Twitter playing pass it on as each student writes parts of the story in 140 characters. Teachers may also have students tweet (post a tweet to Twitter) summaries or key events of stories or chapters in texts read during English language arts. Students may also take on the perspective of a character from a work of fiction read in class, tweet from that characters' perspective, and follow other classmates'

Textbox 7.1.

Focus On:
Digital Write-Backs

Challenge: The use of digital tools makes it easier for students to write more frequently and may increase the amount of writing students produce when using keyboards or touch screens. Although this increase in writing is a positive aspect of using digital tools, more time for grading may be required to respond to and assess all of your students' writing.

Consider: Teachers may take advantage of digital tool functions and participate in digital write-backs with their students by responding to writing via blogging, email, annotation, or direct messaging functions of some educational social networks.

Tips:
1. If students are blogging, select one aspect of the content to respond to and do so in a few quick sentences.
2. Have upper elementary students respond and write back to one another to hold each other accountable, while decreasing your response time.
3. Some social networks, such as Edmodo, allow responses in the form of emoticons to let students know you have read their work and the type of emotion it provoked during reading.
4. Rotate weeks that you respond to a select number of students (e.g., 5–7) so that you respond to all students each month, but a reasonable number per week.
5. Conduct multiple think-alouds while responding to a sample student's writing (with their permission) to model for students what you are looking for in their online writing to decrease the amount of time you spend correcting the content of students' writing during your write-backs.

Check Out: *Edublogs* (www.edublogs.org)

Edublogs allows teachers to create multiple types of blogs, which are secure and easy to use, to integrate into their classroom instruction. These blogs function as excellent digital writing tools that allow for teacher write-backs with students.

---

tweets and respond to those tweets in character. These types of activities allow students to write in a collaborative manner while encouraging students to consider only the most important ideas they wish to convey as Twitter posts are limited in character count.

Remarks on Using Digital Tools to Promote Writing

When engaging students in using digital tools for writing, teachers must consider the amount of student autonomy they wish to promote with lessons. When using any tool that publishes students' writing to the Internet, teachers must be active in monitoring all student posts and gathering parent permission before engaging students in these types of writing. Using websites that are closed or invitation-only creates a safe space for students to write in and express ideas and are a viable option for many classroom teachers to carefully implement online writing into their instruction. Yet, teachers should not readily disregard online tools that are open to other users if they offer unique literacy opportunities. However, rules for using these sites and teacher diligence in monitoring the activity of these sites is imperative.

SAMPLE LESSON PLAN

The following lesson plan (Table 7.1) allows students to collaboratively develop and write a fictional short story in an English language arts class. Students will incorporate the use of images using the Mindnode app to plan and organize their writing. We selected this app because it allows students flexibility in mapping ideas, offers note-making features and ways to embed images within graphic organizers, provides an easy-to-use method of creating graphic organizers and story maps that may be modified, and allows for continuous modification to maps. The Mindnode app is free. If you do not have classroom iPads or tablets, this part of the lesson may be accomplished using paper and colored pencils or small dry erase boards, although you may need to provide a mini-lesson in creating a graphic organizer or provide pre-made graphic organizers for students. However, we note that teacher-prepared graphic organizers might not provide as much flexibility in organizing writing to promote creativity. Titanpad is also a free tool and can be used on any computer. Teachers can sign in to create a class site and then invite students to join the page that is created. As each new user contributes writing to the page, their work shows up in a different color so that teachers and students can easily distinguish who contributed each idea. The page also has a live chat feature that students can use to discuss ideas and ask questions as they

Table 7.1. Sixth Grade Sample Lesson Using Collaborative Tools to Create Shared Writing

Instructional Goals of the lesson:
- Students will create a graphic organizer using tablets to digitally outline and organize a created fiction short story focusing on a studied theme.
- Students will collaborate using TitanPad to write a play.

Common Core Standards Addressed:
CCSS.ELA-Literacy.W.6.3
Write narratives to develop real or imagined experiences or events using effective technique, relevant descriptive details, and well-structured event sequences.
The CCSS.ELA-Literacy.W.6.3 sub-standards A-E are also applicable to this lesson.
CCSS.ELA-Literacy.W.6.4
Produce clear and coherent writing in which the development, organization, and style are appropriate to task, purpose, and audience.
CCSS.ELA-Literacy.W.6.6
Use technology, including the Internet, to produce and publish writing as well as to interact and collaborate with others; demonstrate sufficient command of keyboarding skills to type a minimum of three pages in a single sitting.

English Language Proficiency Standards Addressed:
1. Construct meaning from oral presentations and literary and informational text through grade-appropriate listening, reading, and viewing
3. Speak and write about grade-appropriate complex literary and informational texts and topics
7. Adapt language choices to purpose, task, and audience when speaking and writing
9. Create clear and coherent grade-appropriate speech and text
10. Make accurate use of standard English to communicate in grade-appropriate speech and writing

Lesson Description & Instructional Approach:
The activities in this lesson should be completed in small groups and over multiple classes. Each small group will write one play.
- After reading and studying a short story in the suspense genre (i.e., *The Monkey's Paw* by W. W. Jacobs) and discussing this genre as a class, students will be assigned the task of developing and writing a short story with the same theme. The teacher will group students in small groups of 4 or 5 students, and these groups will serve as writing groups. Each group will create one story.
- The teacher will provide students with a list of literary elements that must be included in the created story (e.g., foreshadowing, conflict). (This element of the lesson may also be more collaborative with the entire class coming up with literary elements that must be included and are particular to the suspense genre.)
- Each group will be given a digital tablet with the Mindnode app installed. The teacher will model planning of the short story using the app by outlining important features of the story, such as characters, setting, and mood, that should be planned before writing. Students will create a graphic organizer story map to outline their story by:

- ° Creating text bubbles or boxes and lines to connect and sort ideas.
- ° Including notes for the text bubbles or boxes to elaborate ideas.
- ° Reorganizing bubbles or boxes as they discuss the outline for story clarity.
- Students will also note within the graphic organizer responsibilities each group member will have in writing the story. For example, students may decide to divide up the story by sections within the outline, with each student writing a part of the story to create a full story.
- After completing the graphic organizer, the teacher will create a TitanPad page for each group, and invite group members to the document. This process will give the teacher access to all stories to provide feedback and monitor students' writing.
- Students will each write their section of the story on the TitanPad page on a computer, reading the text that was already written before writing their own text.
- After stories are complete, students will each take responsibility for refining and editing the text for clarity and precise writing. The teacher may assign students different aspects of the story to edit. For example, one student may be assigned to edit for grammar, one for clarity, one for consistency of plot, and so forth.
- The teacher will then read students' stories and provide feedback through TitanPad.
- Students will read the teachers' comments, confer as a group, and edit their text based on those comments through in-text edits, and response comments explaining how and why revisions were made.

Digital Tools/Apps Used:
- iPad
- Mindnode app
- Computer
- TitanPad

Digital Contribution to Instruction
- Students will practice outlining techniques and manipulation of digital mapping features using Mindnode.
- Students will practice traditional and digital writing skills using TitanPad to create a short story.
- Students practice revising techniques and responding to editorial comments using digital tools.

Potential Constraints
- There may be a learning curve with Mindnode. **Solution**: Allow students time to practice using the app on a simple practice assignment as a class.
- Students may only use Mindnode in a superficial manner by creating an aesthetically pleasing graphic organizer that has little substance. **Solution**: The teacher could require specific elements within the outline, such as images to support ideas or brainstorming notes to accompany text boxes.
- Students will be working in TitanPad at the same time, which may be confusing to students who do not have experience with collaborative tools such as this, and work may be counterproductive. **Solution**: The teacher will model the use of TitanPad and show students how their work will appear in different colors.

(continued)

Table 7.1. (*continued*)

Instructional Considerations

- TitanPad requires a page to be set up. The teacher should set the page up and invite students to join it in advance so that instructional time is not taken up with this aspect of the tool.
- Because TitanPad allows students to interact without being physically near each other, the teacher will need to consider where and how she would like students to work on this project.

Reflection

Now that you have completed this lesson, consider the connections between students' traditional and digital literacy skills. How could both sets of skills be better supported? What aspects of the lesson did students respond most positively to, and how can those aspects be reinforced or supplemented in future lessons merging digital and traditional literacy skills?

work. This lesson plan was developed for sixth grade students, but may be adapted for earlier grades by increasing teacher assistance, modifying this lesson to a whole-class lesson, or allowing students to use images or oral language instead of writing words to organize and create the play.

RESOURCES AND IDEAS FOR INTEGRATING DIGITAL TECHNOLOGY INTO WRITING

Table 7.2 provides additional apps, websites, and teaching ideas for integrating digital technology into your writing instruction.

REFLECTION QUESTIONS

1. What are some of the benefits of collaborative writing online? For what purposes might you have your students write collaboratively?
2. Consider all the ways that students can publish their work online (blogs, social networking sites, websites, etc.). Each outlet has a different purpose and different audience. Brainstorm the ways that you might have students publish their work online. How should the format and content of their writing differ for each outlet?

REFERENCE

Barone, D.M., & Mallette, M.H. (2013). On using twitter. *The Reading Teacher, 66*(5), 377–79.

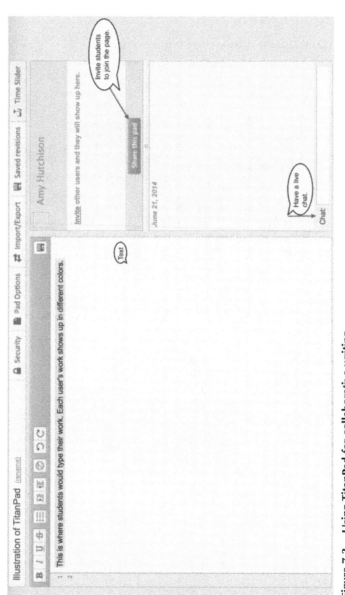

Figure 7.3.   Using TitanPad for collaborative writing.

Table 7.2. Resources and Ideas for Integrating Digital Tools Into Writing Instruction

Digital Resources	Possible Uses	Grade-Specific Examples & CCSS Addressed
Apps: • iWrite Words • Little Writer • Magnetic Alphabet HD • Dragon Dictation • Haiku Poem • Acrostic Poem • Story Patch • Book Creator • Bookemon Mobile • Storyrobe • iDiary for Kids • inClass • Storyboarder Toolbox Online Resources: • www.bubbl.us • www.wordle.net • www.storybird.com • www.storyjumper.com • www.tikatok.com • www.spaghettibookclub.org	Students may: • Practice tracing letters • Practice making words with magnetic letters • Dictate ideas and check dictation for correctness • Create and share poetry • Create and publish books • Pre-write to organize information • Select images from which to create a story	**Kindergarten:** Students may use apps such as Little Writer and iWrite Words to practice writing upper- and lower case letters. **CCSS.ELA-Literacy.L.K.1.A** *Print many upper- and lowercase letters.* **First Grade:** Use the StorySpark class play template on tikatok.com to write a class play. The built-in prompts guide students through the details. **CCSS.ELA-Literacy.W.1.3** *Write narratives in which they recount two or more appropriately sequenced events, include some details regarding what happened, use temporal words to signal event order, and provide some sense of closure.* **CCSS.ELA-Literacy.W.1.6** *With guidance and support from adults, use a variety of digital tools to produce and publish writing, including in collaboration with peers.* **Second Grade:** Have students write online book reviews for the Spaghetti Book Club (www.spaghettibookclub.org). This site requires students to include summaries, detailed opinions with supportive details and examples, and recommendations.

CCSS.ELA-Literacy.W.2.1

Write opinion pieces in which they introduce the topic or book they are writing about, state an opinion, supply reasons that support the opinion, use linking words (e.g., because, and, also) to connect opinion and reasons, and provide a concluding statement.

CCSS.ELA-Literacy.W.2.6

With guidance and support from adults, use a variety of digital tools to produce and publish writing, including in collaboration with peers.

Third Grade: Have students use the iDiary For Kids app to create digital a scrapbook. Students can create entries about their participation in classroom activities and include photos and drawings to accompany their writing.

CCSS.ELA-Literacy.W.3.3

Write narratives to develop real or imagined experiences or events using effective technique, descriptive details, and clear event sequences.

CCSS.ELA-Literacy.W.3.4

With guidance and support from adults, produce writing in which the development and organization are appropriate to task and purpose.

CCSS.ELA-Literacy.W.3.6

With guidance and support from adults, use technology to produce and publish writing (using keyboarding skills) as well as to interact and collaborate with others.

CCSS.ELA-Literacy.W.3.8

Recall information from experiences or gather information from print and digital sources; take brief notes on sources and sort evidence into provided categories.

(continued)

Table 7.2. (continued)

Digital Resources	Possible Uses	Grade-Specific Examples & CCSS Addressed
		CCSS.ELA-Literacy.W.3.10
		Write routinely over extended time frames (time for research, reflection, and revision) and shorter time frames (a single sitting or a day or two) for a range of discipline-specific tasks, purposes, and audiences.
		Fourth Grade: Have students use the inClass app to record data and notes from a science experiment. The app allows users to include video and audio notes and to collaborate and share notes with other app users.
		CCSS.ELA-Literacy.W.4.2
		Write informative/explanatory texts to examine a topic and convey ideas and information clearly.
		CCSS.ELA-Literacy.W.4.4
		Produce clear and coherent writing in which the development and organization are appropriate to task, purpose, and audience.
		CCSS.ELA-Literacy.W.4.6
		With some guidance and support from adults, use technology, as well as to interact and collaborate with others; demonstrate sufficient command of keyboarding skills to type a minimum of one page in a single sitting.
		CCSS.ELA-Literacy.W.4.7
		Conduct short research projects that build knowledge through investigation of different aspects of a topic.
		CCSS.ELA-Literacy.W.4.8
		Recall relevant information from experiences or gather relevant information from print and digital sources; take notes and categorize information, and provide a list of sources.

<u>**CCSS.ELA-Literacy.W.4.10**</u>

Write routinely over extended time frames (time for research, reflection, and revision) and shorter time frames (a single sitting or a day or two) for a range of discipline-specific tasks, purposes, and audiences.

Fifth Grade: Have students use the Storyboarder Toolbox app to create a storyboard for a movie script. They should include captions for each image they select and write a description of each scene.

<u>**CCSS.ELA-Literacy.W.5.3**</u>

Write narratives to develop real or imagined experiences or events using effective technique, descriptive details, and clear event sequences.

<u>**CCSS.ELA-Literacy.W.5.4**</u>

Produce clear and coherent writing in which the development and organization are appropriate to task, purpose, and audience.

<u>**CCSS.ELA-Literacy.W.5.6**</u>

With some guidance and support from adults, use technology, including the internet, to produce and publish writing as well as to interact and collaborate with others; demonstrate sufficient command of keyboarding skills to type a minimum of two pages in a sitting.

<u>**CCSS.ELA-Literacy.W.5.10**</u>

Write routinely over extended time frames (time for research, reflection, and revision) and shorter time frames (a single sitting or a day or two) for a range of discipline-specific tasks, purposes, and audiences.

Sixth Grade: Have students use the Haiku Poem app to create and share Haiku poetry.

(continued)

Table 7.2. *(continued)*

Digital Resources	Possible Uses	Grade-Specific Examples & CCSS Addressed
		CCSS.ELA-Literacy.W.6.4
		Produce clear and coherent writing in which the development, organization, and style are appropriate to task, purpose, and audience.
		W.6.6 - Use technology, including the Internet, to produce and publish writing as well as to interact and collaborate with others; demonstrate sufficient command of keyboarding skills to type a minimum of three pages in a single sitting.
		CCSS.ELA-Literacy.W.6.10
		Write routinely over extended time frames (time for research, reflection, and revision) and shorter time frames (a single sitting or a day or two) for a range of discipline-specific tasks, purposes, and audiences.

Chapter Eight

Reading and Writing Multimodal Text

Thanks to her plan for strategically introducing new tasks and tools, Mrs. Johnson's students have been highly successful in acquiring digital skills. As a result, the students are ready to create more complex multimedia products. This month Mrs. Johnson will help her students learn how to write multimodal compositions. That is, her students will create products that consist of some combination of text, images, video, colors, and sound. Although her students now know how to work with each of these components, it will be essential that Mrs. Johnson teaches them how the combination of these modes of communication influences the meaning of their message. She will need to provide effective examples and models for her students. This month, she will use the Snapguide website to have her students create how-to guides. Through this project, her students will develop important skills for writing instructions while also continuing to use the digital tools and skills they have already developed.

Imagine you have just relocated to a new town, and you are interested in finding the best coffee shop the town has to offer. The first step you might take will be to conduct a quick Internet search to find listings of local coffee shops. After pulling up a list of coffee shops, you click on the name of a shop, Local Coffee, close to your home. Once directed to the Local Coffee website, you have the opportunity to read about the origins of the coffee shop, watch a video on local trade coffee, and view a menu of the shop's coffee offerings, all the while listening to a sample of music often played in this coffee shop. Before even seeing the coffee shop in person or entering its doors, you understand the atmosphere, mood, and products offered by Local Coffee. Thus, the website served as a type of informational text in which you gathered information to understand a topic (in this case, the coffee shop). Now, consider how your knowledge and understanding about Local Coffee might be different if you only had a paper flier in which to gather information about the shop.

The advent of presenting and sharing information in a digital format has prompted a change in the way in which information is composed and understood. These compositions often incorporate multiple modes of reading and writing, including sound, images, colors, videos, and/or animations, and are aptly termed multimodal compositions. The chapters thus far have focused on one particular mode of reading or writing. We turn in this chapter to the incorporation of multiple modes to consider how you might incorporate multimodal composition into your own K-6 classrooms. We consider multimodal composition to be important because giving students the power to represent their ideas and thinking using various modes of communication provides opportunities for them to display both their knowledge and application of their knowledge (Jewitt, 2008).

COMMON CORE CONNECTIONS

Multimodal composition is also represented in the Common Core State Standards. Although the CCSS calls for students to use technology to publish and interact with others (CCSS.ELA-Literacy.CCRA.W.6), indicating composition that goes beyond writing in a Word document, other writing standards can readily be addressed using multimodal composition. For example, for students to "write informative/explanatory texts to examine and convey complex ideas" (CCSS.ELA-Literacy.CCRA.W.2) they must draw on multiple types of knowledge and produce work that represents the complexity of their knowledge. By using multiple modes of writing and composing, students may effectively display their knowledge of complex ideas. Digital tools offer students multiple means to do so with platforms of composition that combine auditory, visual, and written text. Using these platforms to compose also aligns with CCSS anchor standards focused on speaking and listening, such as having students "integrate and evaluate information presented in diverse media and formats, including visually, quantitatively, and orally" (CCSS. ELA-Literacy.CCRA.SL.2). By doing so, students will also use digital tools strategically to express information in a manner that highlights understanding of topics (CCSS.ELA-Literacy.CCRA.SL.5). This sample of anchor standards highlights the importance of incorporating multimodal composition into classroom instruction, and we provide ideas and sample tools in the following sections for you to think about practical applications of digital tools to engage your students in composing multimodal texts.

MULTIMODAL TOOLS IN THE CLASSROOM

Screencasting

Screencasting takes place when a user captures the action on a computer screen while narrating. Screencasts are multimodal tools that record everything on the computer screen while also capturing the accompanying sound. Therefore, screencasts can be used to illustrate anything that you would like to show someone on a computer screen. Screencasts can be recording with screencasting tools such as Jing (www.techsmith.com/jing.html), Screenr (www.screenr.com), Screencast-O-Matic (www.screencast-o-matic.com), and Screen Toaster (www.gigaom.com). These are all free tools that vary in the features they offer. Although Google Hangout is a video conferencing tool, it can also capture and record the audio and action on the screen during a Hangout, thus creating a screencast.

Screencasting can be useful to both teachers and students. Teachers can record screencasts to explain a concept, capture lectures, highlight information on a website, provide a tutorial, or even illustrate how to use a digital tool. By creating screencasts, students will be able to watch the teacher's tutorial or explanation at any time, in school or out of school, and even re-watch an illustration when they need extra assistance. Teachers can also use screencasts to provide feedback on student work. One useful aspect of screencasting for this purpose is that the teacher can show the student's work on the screen and highlight specific parts of the work. Another potential use of screencasts is for teachers to create videos for parents that illustrate what the students are working on in class or how to practice a particular comprehension strategy with a child so that the parents can continue the work at home.

Students can also record screencasts to illustrate their understanding, explain their thinking, or create an informational presentation. For example, students may record a screencast as they read information on a website and explain their thinking as they read the information. This type of screencast can help teachers see how students read online, how they make sense of all the different types of text (image, video, hyperlinks, etc.), and what type of instruction students may still need in regards to reading and navigating websites. Students can also create screencasts to create a summary of what they have read or studied, to explain an image, to give directions, to talk about their understanding of a text, or to ask questions about a text. There are numerous possibilities for any type of activity in which students or teachers would benefit from seeing the work taking place on a screen.

Creating and Watching Tutorials

Asking students to create their own tutorials for an outside audience is a great way to have students search for, learn, and apply information about a topic using multimodalities. One beneficial way to both watch and create educational tutorials is through the ShowMe app for iPad (www.showme.com). The creators describe ShowMe as a global learning community where anyone can learn or teach anything. This app allows users to watch lessons that have been added by users and are organized by topic. For example, there are categories such as grammar, writing, spelling, and poetry. Within those categories you can find lessons on everything from writing a summary to learning about different word families. This app also allows the user to create their own lesson tutorials by combining images, writing, color, and audio recording. The user can then categorize and share their tutorial with others through the ShowMe site. Other tools that we like for creating or watching tutorials on a variety of topics include Explain Everything (www.morriscooke.com) and Screenchomp (www.techsmith.com/screenchomp.html).

Collaborative Presentation and Discussion

Another valuable use of digital tools that allows for multiple modes of communication is the use of digital tools for creating collaborative presentations and promoting discussion. There are many tools that allow the user to upload and narrate presentations and elicit feedback and discussion. One example is VoiceThread (www.voicethread.com). VoiceThread is a tool that allows the user to upload, share and discuss documents, presentations, images, audio files, and videos. With VoiceThread, you can also annotate images and text on the screen. By sharing a VoiceThread, you can invite users to respond to the shared work by responding with audio, video, or standard text replies for each slide of the VoiceThread presentation. Everyone who views the VoiceThread presentation can also see or hear all of the responses for the presentation. See http://voicethread.com/about/library/all_about_polar_bears/ for an example of a VoiceThread created in a Kindergarten class, or http://voicethread.com/about/library/3rd_Grade_from_Alice_Mercer/ for a third-grade example.

Students can also combine audio with images to engage in what Hutchison (2014) calls Multimodal Explanatory Composition. This strategy consists of students combining text, images, and audio to explain their understanding of an informational text. There are many tools that that facilitate this type of response. Some of our favorite ways of doing this are with Educreations (www.educreations.com), Glogster (www.glogster.com), Doodlecast Pro (www.doodlecastpro.com), and Knovio (www.knovio.com). Each of these

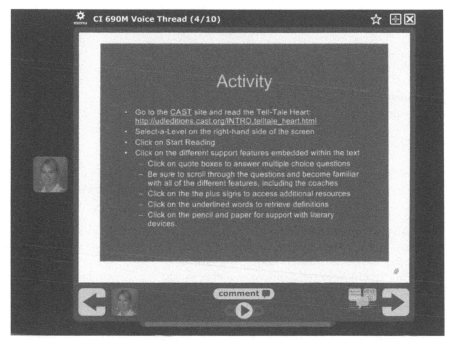

Figure 8.1. Example of Activity Presented Using VoiceThread.

tools allow the user to combine audio, images, words, and links to additional resources such as videos. Knovio also allows the user to record a video to accompany the presentation. An example of a multimodal explanatory composition activity might be to have students read a text and explain their understanding of the main ideas in a text with Educreations. With Educreations, the student could draw, write, and use photos or images from the web to explain their ideas. Below, we offer ideas about planning for multimodal composition in instruction in textbox 8.1.

Planning and Creating Videos to Express an Idea, Communicate a Viewpoint, or Respond to a Text or Prompt

Multimodal presentation tools can also be used to simply create videos as a way of expressing ideas, communicating a point of view, responding to a text, or responding to a prompt. This idea differs from the previous discussions in that the students would not create a presentation, but rather, a video. Creating simple videos are a quick and easy alternative to creating presentations because they are efficient and do not require planning. Students can quickly capture their thoughts and ideas with a video. Although screencasts, tutorials,

---

Textbox 8.1.

Focus On:
Planning for Multimodal Composition

Challenge: Although multimodal composition offers students various modes to express their ideas and explain information, planning for this type of composition can be complex as multiple types of digital technology must be considered and prepared for in instruction.

Consider: Sometimes project-based activities that span multiple class meetings allow for easier implementation of several digital tools.

Tips:
1. When first introducing students to multimodal composition, focus only on two modes of communication (e.g., audio and image) to allow students to adapt to this new form of composing text.
2. Particularly in lower-elementary grades, spend ample time familiarizing students with each type of digital tool they will use to compose.
3. Allow students opportunities to "play" with the digital tools in low-risk, non-assessed settings.
4. In upper-elementary grades, partner students together to create multimodal compositions as they can learn from one another and support one another. Consider teacher-led small group work in lower-elementary grades.
5. Have students create a multimodal composition about a topic with which they are highly familiar. For example, after students spend a unit studying conflict in fiction, have them create a multimodal story that includes a conflict.

Check Out: National Council of Teachers of English (NCTE) *Strategic Policy Goals* regarding multimodal literacies and technologies (http://www.ncte.org/governance/multimodalliteracies)

Learn more about multimodal composition and multimodalities outlined by NCTE and what these goals mean for teaching and learning.

---

and multimodal explanatory compositions are much more inclusive and thorough, a video can provide quick insight into students' ideas when needed and appropriate. YouTube is one of the simplest tools for recording and sharing a video. With YouTube, the user can click "upload" to record a video from a webcam and instantly share or embed the link. Students can also use small, hand-held video cameras to interview one another on a topic to convey reactions to texts and to practice questioning skills using multimodalities.

Animation

Students may also enjoy creating alternative types of responses such as Blabbers, which are animations that are appealing, particularly for young students, for response. Blabberize (www.blabberize.com) allows students to animate an image of a person, animal, object, or a drawing. One way of using Blabberize is to create a story told from a particular character's point of view. The student can then read the story and create an image of the character to make it appear as though the character is speaking. Visit http://bit.ly/TqJmuK to see examples of third graders' stories written from a dog's point of view and then animated with Blabberize to make it appear as though the dog is telling the story. Students may enjoy this type of activity because it varies from traditional language arts activities and allows students creativity in using traditional literacies, such as oral and retelling skills. Similarly, with Voki (www. voki.com), students and teachers can create speaking characters to express their ideas. The site allows the user to customize an avatar and create audio messages with it. This site also provides an option to use Voki Classroom, a learning management system that allows students to use their avatars to create and submit work online.

For younger students, Puppet Pals (http://bit.ly/1jTQsPV) is a promising tool for animated storytelling. The Puppet Pals app allows students to select characters and back drops that can be moved around as the student tells a story. The movements and audio are recorded in real time so that the story can be played back later. Students must make decisions to create the setting for the story, which again reinforces traditional literacies using digital tools. Similarly, Toontastic (http://www.launchpadtoys.com/toontastic/) allows users to create and share cartoons and is another option for multimodal storytelling and presentation.

Multimedia and Interactive Presentation Tools

Although presentation tools, such as PowerPoint, often evoke images of meaningless work with too much text on each slide, these types of tools can be used for an array of meaningful classroom activities. The value of the activity depends on the work that is assigned by the teacher. An important aspect of presentation tools is that they can help students learn how to make intentional choices with the colors, font, and images they select to convey their message, as each of these textual components convey meaning. Additionally, interactive presentation tools, such as Doceri (www.doceri.com) can help engage and create opportunities for responsive instruction and interaction. Doceri not only allows users to create presentations, but also

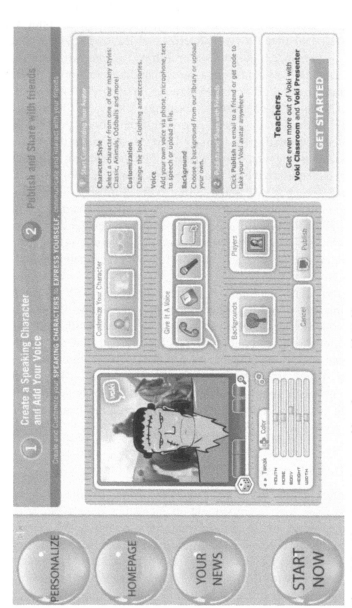

Figure 8.2.   How to create a speaking character with Voki.

allows users to annotate existing PDFs and presentations on an iPad while also projecting the information live. Thus, this tool is useful for both teachers and students.

Examples of other tools that help students create engaging presentations that convey their understanding of a topic or idea include Prezi (www.prezi. com), Haiku Deck (www.haikudeck.com), and Snapguide (www.snapguide. com). Snapguide allows the user to create and share a how-to guide in the form of a presentation that combines images or videos with text. For example, a popular guide in this site is titled *How to Give a Hedgehog a Bath*. This type of presentation would be useful to combine with an informational writing activity. Students could create informational guides on topics of interest, as guides can be posted and shared by topic. Some examples of topics on the site that would likely be appealing to students include games, pets, sports, and music.

Other tools for conveying information are sites that allow interactive and collaborative posting such as Padlet (www.padlet.com) and Primary Wall (www.primarywall.com). These sites allow multiple users to contribute to a shared virtual wall space. This type of tool can be used to collaboratively construct a presentation or share ideas on a topic, and everyone's activity on the wall can be instantly seen. Users can add links and documents to their posts, or use a built in camera to take and add a photo. The walls can easily be saved to various formats and shared, and can also be embedded into other sites such as class blogs. Padlet also generates a QR code for accessing the wall. Figure 8.3 shows an image of a shared wall created with Padlet.

Storing and Sharing Videos and Other Multimedia Productions

In addition to tools for creating videos and other multimodal presentations, teachers will need a method and tool for storing and sharing them. Vimeo (www.vimeo.com) is a video storage site that allows users to store videos and make them private. This is a good option for teachers because Vimeo interfaces with many iPad apps, allowing the users to save their video from within an iPad app to the password protected video storage site. YouTube also allows users to store videos to private, password-protected accounts. Even if a video is not created with YouTube, it can be uploaded to the site and the user gets to choose whether the video is accessible to others.

In addition to videos, there are also sites for storing and sharing presentations, documents, PDFs, and infographics. Slideshare (www.slideshare.net) is one of the most popular sites for storing and sharing this type of content and is currently the world's largest online community for sharing presentations and

The brain uses over a quarter of the oxygen used by the human body.
-By John

Most adults have 32 teeth.
-Krissy

It takes the body around 12 hours to completely digest eaten food.
-Katie

Interesting Facts About the Human Body: Check out this site!

Science Kids
Fun science & technology for kids

Science Facts

Human Body Facts

As well as having unique fingerprints, humans also have unique tongue prints.
Jason

Your nose and ears continue growing throughout your entire life.
-Amy

The left side of your body is controlled by the right side of your brain while the right side of your body is controlled by the left side of your brain.
-Chris

Figure 8.3. Shared Wall Created With Padlet.

professional content. Users can upload content of their own and also search content by topic.

SAMPLE LESSON PLAN

This lesson plan example involves the use of Snapguide for writing and presenting explanatory text in a multimodal format. Snapguide, as we noted previously, can be used on the web or as an iPad app. Snapguide is a free app and web service that allows users to create and share step-by-step "how to" guides. The lesson plan uses first grade CCSS writing standards.

Table 8.1. Sample First-grade Lesson Plan Using Snapguide to Publish an Informational Text

Instructional Goals of the Lesson:
Students will write a how-to guide and illustrate and present it with a Snapguide presentation.

Common Core Standards Addressed:
CCSS.ELA-LITERACY.W.1.7
Participate in shared research and writing projects (e.g., explore a number of "how-to" books on a given topic and use them to write a sequence of instructions).
CCSS.ELA-LITERACY.W.1.6
With guidance and support from adults, use a variety of digital tools to produce and publish writing, including in collaboration with peers.

English Language Proficiency Standards Addressed:
3. Speak and write about grade-appropriate complex literary and informational texts and topics
7. Adapt language choices to purpose, task, and audience when speaking and writing
9. Create clear and coherent grade-appropriate speech and text

Lesson Description & Instructional Approach:
- To begin this lesson, the teacher should present a mini-lesson on writing a sequence of instructions by showing multiple picture books that are written this way as models. The teacher should also find a guide on Snapguide.com that would be interesting to the students to provide an illustration of a digital how-to guide.
- The teacher should model the creation of a how-to guide on Snapguide to help students understand the kind of writing they will be doing.
- The teacher should then provide students with a selection of relevant topics for which to create how-to guides. Some examples include getting dressed, how to ride a scooter, how to care for a pet, or how to get your mom or caregiver to give you your favorite food for dinner.

(continued)

Table 8.1. (*continued*)

- Students will begin by using a digital graphic organizer, such as Popplet, to list the steps for their how-to guide. By using a digital organizer, the student will be able to copy and paste the text into Snapguide when they are ready to create their presentation. At this stage, the students should also list what kind of image they would like to accompany the text. Students can use the built-in camera on a tablet or computer to takes pictures for their presentation. We recommend limiting the students to a small number of steps (3–5) if this is their first time creating a how-to guide and/or creating a Snapguide.
- Students should then create their Snapguide presentation by going to the Snapguide app or website. Once on the site, it is simple to create presentations following these steps:
  - Click "Create a Guide."
  - Type a title for the guide.
  - Click on the cover of the guide to insert a photo and add text.
  - Click "add steps" to continue adding steps. Students can then copy and paste their work from their graphic organizer to add their steps to the guide. Students can also insert pictures from the built-in camera at this point.
  - Once all steps are complete, the student chooses a category for the guide and then clicks "publish" to share the work.
  - Once created, the guide can be shared in multiple ways, including by embedding it into another site such as a class blog, and can be printed.
- Once all guides are published, students should review each other's guides and make comments (guided by the teacher) using the comments feature on the site.

Digital Devices and Tools Used
- An iPad or computer
- Digital Graphic Organizer Such as Popplet
- Built-in camera on a computer or iPad
- Snapguide website or app (www.snapguide.com)

Digital Contribution to Instruction
- By creating a Snapguide, students are:
  - learning how to match images and text
  - creating a guide with a real audience in mind
  - gaining experience using a digital graphic organizer, using a built-in camera, and navigating a new tool

Potential Constraints
- Snapguide only accepts images saved in jpeg format. **Solution:** Check in advance the format in which images are saved on the devices your students will be using. If images are not automatically saved to the correct format, show students how to save them to a jpeg format.
- The site will allow you to create a guide without having an account or signing in. However, you cannot publish the guide without signing in. **Solution:** Create a class account for all students to use.
- If you are not signed into the site when you begin creating the guide, you will be taken through a tutorial each time you create a guide. Students may have difficulty navigating through this. **Solution:** Have all students sign in using the class account before they begin their work.

- Students may have difficulty going between multiple apps/sites and copying and pasting their work. **Solution:** Carefully model this for the students. If using an iPad, show students the feature that allows them to swipe four fingers across the screen to go back and forth between apps.

Instructional Considerations
- Because students will be using a digital organizer instead of a paper-based organizer, you may wish to provide students with a structure for the organizer since tools like Popplet let the user create the structure. Since leaning how to create graphic organizers is not the focus of this lesson, showing students how to lay out their organizer may help the lesson go more quickly and be less confusing for students.
- Students may need to walk around the room or building to take photos for their guide. Consider how you will manage this aspect of the lesson. Consider setting boundaries in advance.
- If you are not using a mobile device, students will only be able to include pictures that can be captured from a stationary desktop camera. Therefore, this limitation may influence the topics you allow students to select. Alternately, you may choose to let students find pictures online.
- The teacher will need to consider in what ways he or she would like students to share and publish the work.

Reflection
After conducting the lesson, consider the extent to which you were able to adhere to your instructional goal. What helped or hindered your students' abilities to meet the instructional goal? Note what you may need to do differently the next time you use these technologies.

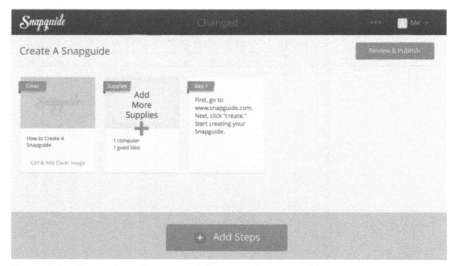

Figure 8.4. Screenshot of process used to create a Snapguide.

Table 8.2. Resources for Integrating Digital Tools for Multimodal Composing

Digital Resources	Possible Uses	Grade-Specific Examples & CCSS Addressed
Apps: • Doceri • Puppet Pals • ScreenChomp • ScreenToaster • ShowMe • Toontastic **Online Resources:** • Biteslide (www.biteslide.com) • Blabberize (www.blabberize.com) • Educreations (www.educreations. com) • Explain Everything (www. morriscooke.com) • Glogster (www.glogster.com) • Haiku Deck (www.haikudeck.com) • Jing (www.techsmith.com/jing) • Knovio (www.knovio.com) • Mashable (www.mashable.com)	Students may: • Annotate screen content using narration • Create presentations using words, images, audio, and video • Create and share video tutorials • Create and share slide-show presentations • Study student-created tutorials • Create and record audiovisual stories with animation • Develop collaborative presentations • Give and receive audiovisual feedback • Combine images, video, and audio to create multimodal texts • Create videos for presentation of ideas or stories and share those videos online • Engage in perspective-taking using animated avatars • Create multimedia timelines	**Kindergarten:** With guidance and support from a teacher, a kindergarten class could collaboratively create a class play or story using an animation-based audiovisual online program or app and publish that text online. **CCSS.ELA-Literacy.W.K.3.** *Use a combination of drawing, dictating, and writing to narrate a single event or several loosely linked events, tell about the events in the order in which they occurred, and provide a reaction to what happened.* **CCSS.ELA-Literacy.W.K.6.** *With guidance and support from adults, explore a variety of digital tools to produce and publish writing, including in collaboration with peers.* **First Grade:** Students may collaboratively develop, with assistance from a teacher, a Glog (using Glogster) to explain the life-cycle of a butterfly.

CCSS.ELA-Literacy.W.1.2. *Write informative/explanatory texts in which they name a topic, supply some facts about the topic, and provide some sense of closure.*

Second Grade: *A second-grade class may interact with their teacher using a real-time online whiteboard to respond to prompts, answer questions, and share notes and ideas about a story read during English language arts.*

CCSS.ELA-Literacy.SL.2.1. *Participate in collaborative conversations with diverse partners about grade 2 topics and texts with peers and adults in small and larger groups.*

Third Grade: Students could use an online photo sharing resource with voice and text annotation capabilities to explain types of volcanoes and volcano eruptions.

CCSS.ELA-Literacy.SL.3.2. *Determine the main ideas and supporting details of a text read aloud or information presented in diverse media and formats, including visually, quantitatively, and orally.*

Fourth Grade: Students may create an audiovisual time line using a digital timeline creator (e.g., Tiki-toki) to textually, visually, and orally develop and annotate a timeline of the voyage and sinking of the Titanic.

(continued)

Teachers may:
- Create screencast tutorials to provide extended learning opportunities
- Provide audio feedback to student work
- Search and find tutorials to include in instruction
- Capture students' thinking
- Store students' digital artifacts
- Work with students in real time on an online interactive white board
- Create teacher avatars to provide students with online tutorials

- Prezi (www.prezi.com)
- Primary Wall (www.primarywall.com)
- Screenr (www.screenr.com)
- Screencast-o-matic (www.screencast-o-matic.com)
- Slideshare (www.slideshare.net)
- Snapguide (www.snapguide.com)
- Tiki-toki (www.tiki-toki.com)
- Vimeo (www.vimeo.com)
- VoiceThread (www.voicethread.com)
- Voki (www.voki.com)
- Youtube (www.youtube.com)

Table 8.2. (continued)

Digital Resources	Possible Uses	Grade-Specific Examples & CCSS Addressed
		CCSS.ELA-Literacy.W.4.2. *Write informative/ explanatory texts to examine a topic and convey ideas and information clearly.* **CCSS.ELA-Literacy.W.4.2.b.** *Develop the topic with facts, definitions, concrete details, quotations, or other information and examples related to the topic.*
		Fifth Grade: Students could create an online diagram or figure comparing two characters from literature and use a screen-capture tool to orally explain and describe differences using information from the text.
		CCSS.ELA-Literacy.RL.5.3. *Compare and contrast two or more characters, settings, or events in a story or drama, drawing on specific details in the text (e.g., how characters interact).*
		Sixth Grade: Students may upload a visual representation of a literary character to an interactive whiteboard and screencasting tool or app and annotate the representation to describe characteristics and important ideas about that figure to create an explanatory multimodal text.
		CCSS.ELA-Literacy.W.6.2. Write informative/ explanatory texts to examine a topic and convey ideas, concepts, and information through the selection, organization, and analysis of relevant content.

RESOURCES

We provide Table 8.2 to outline different digital resources available for integrating multimodal composition into K-6 instruction. As you peruse this table think about the various ways you could incorporate these resources into your classroom, how you may modify the examples we provide, and how these resources may supplement your current instruction.

REFLECTION QUESTIONS

1. Review a selection of the educational tutorials on the same topic provided on the ShowMe website (www.showme.com). How do the colors, sounds, and images used influence your understanding of the topic? How can you use your observations to help students create effective multimodal presentations?
2. When might it be more effective for students to create multimodal compositions that include more than just text rather than just writing a text-only response?

REFERENCES

Hutchison, A. (2014). Using the Multimodal Explanatory Composition Strategy to Respond to Informational Texts. In Rasinski, T., K. Pytash, & R. Ferdig (Eds.). The Use of Technology in the Teaching of Reading. Bloomington: Solution Tree.

Jewitt, C. (2008). Multimodality and literacy in school classrooms. *Review of Research in Education, 32,* 241–67.

Chapter Nine

Social Media and
Collaboration in the Classroom

Now that Mrs. Johnson's students have begun creating informative and interesting digital products, she wants them to be able to share their work more broadly and to make connections with others on topics of interest. Accordingly, this month she will introduce her students to some social media sites that can facilitate their academic interests. Mrs. Johnson's instructional coach told her about a site called Storify that will allow students to gather information that is posted through different types of social media to create a comprehensive narrative on a topic of interest. Mrs. Johnson knows that it can be difficult to protect students' privacy when they use social media. However, she hopes to overcome this difficulty by creating class accounts that the students can use for various social media sites. She will also provide them with guidelines about how to safely use social media sites.

Although the thought of elementary school-aged children engaging with social media may seem unwarranted or controversial, there are many ways that social media can support children's learning. Like many educators, we believe that children need to have strong oral communication skills and still need to have what might be considered old-fashioned letter-writing skills. However, much of the social interaction in our world today takes place through social media, and with social media comes concerns about digital citizenship and digital safety. Because of these concerns, and also because of the many affordances of social media, we believe that engaging with social media also has a place in the school curriculum. Further, social media can be used to engage students with an audience outside the walls of the classroom and can give students an outlet for developing their voice.

There are many types of social media, but the most widely recognized include social networking sites (such as Facebook), blogs and microblogs (such as Twitter), content communities (such as YouTube and Flickr), collaborative projects (such as Wikipedia), and massive multiplayer online games (such as *World of Warcraft*). Each of these types of social media have different purposes that could be useful to address various aspects of learning in classrooms.

An advantage of social media is that it can provide outsiders with a window into the classroom through content such as Twitter posts and YouTube videos. This connection may be useful for parents who want to know more about what and how their child is learning in school, for other educators looking for creative teaching ideas or ways to inspire students, or for students in other countries interested in how students learn across the world. Social media tools can also help students connect with community members, authors, scientists, and other people of interest to learn more about a topic or project.

Although there may be fears about children's online safety when it comes to social media, these may be assuaged with sites that are created specifically for school-aged children in order to protect their identity and limit their network. Examples of social networking sites created for students include Twiducate and Edmodo. These tools provide a safe space for students and teachers to connect and collaborate. There are also blog sites created specifically for students (such as Kidblog) and other sites offer privacy settings to protect content (such as YouTube) or allow users to post information anonymously.

Beyond what might be considered typical social media sites, there are many tools that allow users to collaborate and share ideas through shared digital spaces. These types of tools can also extend learning beyond the classroom and will also be featured in this chapter. Examples of sites that facilitate collaboration include course management systems (such as Moodle and Gooru), video conferencing tools (such as Skype and Google Hangout), collaborative sticky notes and walls (such as Noteapp and Wallwisher), collaborative Notepads (such as TitanPad and Google Docs) and collaborative drawing boards (such as Scribblar).

COMMON CORE CONNECTIONS

The type of collaboration and interaction supported by social media is also represented in the Common Core State Standards. For example Standard CCSS.ELA-LITERACY.CCRA.W.6 states that students should "use technology, including the Internet, to produce and publish writing and to interact and collaborate with others." Though this is the most obvious standard that could be addressed with social media, there are many other related standards as well. For example Standard CCSS.ELA-LITERACY.CCRA.SL.1, which states "Prepare for and participate effectively in a range of conversations and collaborations with diverse partners, building on others' ideas and expressing their own clearly and persuasively," could be addressed by having students use Skype to discuss a topic with students in another school. In accordance with Standard CCSS.ELA-LITERACY.CCRA.SL.5, social media could also be used to express information. These are just a few of the ways that social media can be used to address Common Core Standards, but there are many more. Engaging students with social media provides an opportunity to teach students about digital citizenship and how to interact safely online. We now turn to how social media can be used in the classroom and how it promotes collaboration within and outside of classroom walls.

SOCIAL MEDIA AND COLLABORATION IN THE CLASSROOM

Often, when we think of the term social media in the classroom, we think about platforms such as Facebook and Twitter that have been gaining popularity in K-12 instruction. Although these platforms are viable options for inciting creativity and connectivity, many other types of digital tools may be used to incorporate social media and collaboration into curricula and we discuss those tools in this section.

Idea Sharing and Building Repositories of Information

Perhaps one of the most popular and powerful reasons to include social media in the K-6 classroom is to allow our students to connect with one another to promote collaborative learning and idea sharing. One way that students may connect with one another to share ideas is through social bookmarking websites, such as Diigo (www.diigo.com) and Delicious (www.delicious.com) that allow users to save web resources, which become known as bookmarks, to a common shared space by copying and pasting the URL of the web resource to the social bookmarking site, creating a bookmark, and annotating the bookmark to describe why it is useful. For example, upper-level elementary students may engage in a research project on Abraham Lincoln and post bookmarks with useful information and images on Diigo. Because Diigo is a social media platform, all of the students in the class would have access to the bookmarks and annotations. Diigo is also a closed network, so the teacher would only grant access to members of the class to form a safe online environment for sharing.

As we discussed in a previous chapter, social media may also be used for collaborative writing. We have discussed how lengthier, more formal writing may be easily managed using TitanPad (see the Lesson Plan in chapter 7) and Google Docs. We also recommend Dropbox (www.dropbox.com) for a similar sharing of documents that can be readily shared and edited among a group of students. To extend these formal class writing exercises in a shared space that can be accessed, if the teacher so desires, by outside audiences, we recommend wiki websites, such as Wikispaces (www.wikispaces.com), as easy-to-use sites that allow classes to create a page of information that becomes shared media. Continuing with the Abraham Lincoln example, after students complete research on President Lincoln, they may compile their learned knowledge into a wiki, instead of a more traditional report, to form a class wiki biography that may be accessed by parents and other classes. Research has suggested that students may be more conscientious of their writing and mechanics of writing when writing on public spaces for audiences besides the teacher (Hutchison & Wang, 2012), indicating another benefit of using wikis to promote idea sharing and collaboration among classes to produce information.

We also like more informal tools such as JustPaste.it (www.justpaste.it) and Primary Wall (www.primarywall.com) to have students write short post-it length notes that can easily be accessed by others. Primary Wall is a great example of this type of collaborative learning. This tool is particularly useful because it can support real-time interaction between teachers and students. Teachers can post prompts on a digital sticky note, and students can respond by typing on the note, reinforcing thinking and writing skills. The teacher can also move the sticky notes around to discuss ideas while students watch on their computer screens or on a classroom smartboard. Figure 9.1 shows a screenshot of a sample Primary Wall.

Another sticky-note digital tool that we have found useful for student collaboration and note making is NoteApp (www.noteapp.com). This platform allows students to write on digital sticky notes about a topic and share those notes with others in the class or in a small group through invitation to their notes.

Indeed, social media is also gaining ground as a popular method for engaging students in discussion and classroom activities to share information and collaborate on school work. Several websites have been developed specifically for the K-12 education sector to support this type of instruction and interaction. Haiku Learning (www.haikulearning.com), Edmodo (www.edmodo.com), and Gooru (www.goorulearning.org) were all developed to help students engage in learning in and out of the classroom. Often referred to as digital learning platforms, these sites allow students to engage online in instruction and discussion similar to that of a physical classroom. All of these sites are free for teachers. Edmodo is a platform, similar in format to Facebook, that offers discussion boards, assignment links that students may

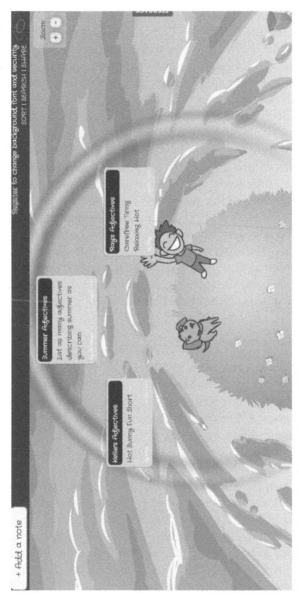

Figure 9.1. Example of using Primary Wall.

use to turn in homework, a digital book bag for students to store files, communication tools, and a class library for the teacher to upload documents that all students can access. Edmodo also allows parents to view, but not participate in, class assignments. Haiku Learning offers a more advanced platform of learning that has the features of Edmodo, with other options like creating class wikis, a database of educational web resources to easily link to the class page, and an e-portfolio feature for students to create portfolios of work. Both platforms are designed for K-12 learning, so we encourage you to check them out and see which might fit your classroom needs and goals. Figure 9.2 shows an example of the Edmodo interface.

Gooru is also a digital learning platform, but it focuses more on accessing, collecting, organizing, and sharing videos and learning content with students to supplement and extend their classroom learning. Teachers may create clusters of information for students to view online and assessments to measure students' learning during these activities. Thus, Gooru is an important multimedia platform to present ideas and information to students through a shared network of learning resources created by educators and customized by you for your classroom and students. If you wish to create your own multimedia platform with original materials you develop, consider creating a Google + (www.plus.google.com) site that you can invite your students (and parents) to visit and engage in learning activities completely designed by you.

Collaboration to Promote Creativity

Social media can also be used to engage students in activities that support creativity, often sparked by collaboration inherent to using social web resources. Digital tools that incorporate images and video on a collaborative platform provide opportunities for students to express knowledge, understanding, or thinking about a topic creatively to share with a larger audience. Photo sharing apps and sites, such as Flickr (www.flickr.com), Instagram (www.instagram.com), and Picasa (www.picasa.google.com) can be used to take and share images with captions and also to search other users' images. For example, students can create a digital field trip after visiting a historical or scientific locale. Because these sites are social and people share photos through them, students can also access other peoples' images of important sites and locations to create a digital field trip without leaving the classroom, if funding is limited. Many of these photo sharing sites also link to Google + or other social media platforms for students to share their digital field trips within a class site. Or, in upper-elementary grades, you may have your students create videos to creatively express knowledge, and share these videos on YouTube (www.youtube.com), with parental permission.

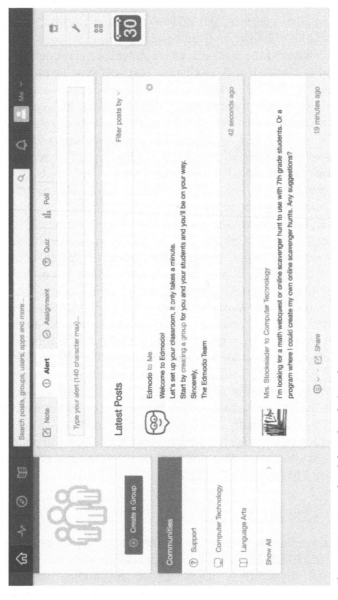

Figure 9.2. Example of the Edmodo interface.

You may also want to try a closed, invite-only social media platform to inspire students to take on different perspectives and post comments and resources in the mindset of a character in fiction or figure in history. Twiducate (www.twiducate.com) is an education platform that functions similarly to Twitter and allows teachers and students to post micro-blog posts to share with a class. Unlike Twitter, only students with the class code, provided by the teacher, can access the platform, although teachers can connect their students with other classes if they so choose. Teachers may use micro-blogging as early as first-grade for students to take on the perspective of a character they read in a story and post comments that they think the character would make based on their understanding of the story. Students can also micro-blog about classroom events (e.g., getting a class pet, conducting a science experiment), which promotes digital and traditional literacy skills. We recommend visiting teacher professional development social sites, such as Edutopia (www.edutopia.com), or following these sites on Twitter for more ideas about using micro-blogging in the elementary classroom.

A final idea for incorporating social media into the elementary classroom to inspire creativity is through gaming. We briefly mentioned *World of Warcraft* as one potential outlet through which students take on roles and use reading and writing skills to play an online game. Such games are also useful to prompt perspective taking because the game is characterized as Massively Multiplayer Online Roleplay (MMOR); thus, students must become a character within the game and interact with others in that character mindset. If, however, you want to consider a non-war-inspired version of gaming to socially engage your students in literacy, consider Second Life (www.secondlife.com) to create your own classroom virtual environment that can place students in the roles of anything from fictional characters to historical figures to themselves in scenarios you prompt to assess student understanding of classroom content. Finally, we suggest looking at Brainpop (www.brainpop.com), which offers a host of social games for students to practice skills from ELA to mathematics. This site also offers videos and other classroom resources useful to teachers of all grades.

Connecting with the Outside World

Social digital media was created for interaction with other people in a way that complements real-life interaction. Connecting with the outside world and people not physically in the same room or building popularized this form of communication and sharing, and this connection may be important for your students to engage in literacy and learning as well. Platforms that allow students to write opinions, post created videos, or summarize learning and then solicit feedback from others engages students in online conversation about their ideas and extends learning beyond a quiz or reflection that only the teacher reads. Blog sites such as Blogger (www.blogger.com) and Edublogs (www.edublogs.com) offer free platforms for students to express their opinions and for others to comment on this writing. Students can make these sites private so that only people with their blog URL can access them. For security, we suggest providing a selected audience to read and respond to your students' blog posts. Perhaps university students studying to become teachers may be interested in blogging with your students, as Colwell (2012) suggested. Simply having students respond to each others' blogs can also be beneficial to extend writing and thinking skills (McGrail & Davis, 2011), and you may find another teacher's class in your district or school that will collaborate on such a project with your class. Another idea is to connect with teachers in different states using professional development websites, which are listed in the resource table. Possible projects excellent for collaborative blogging include discussing reactions to fiction and media, informal debate about current event topics, and practicing expository writing to learn about another person.

If you are interested in connecting your students with other students in another country or state, ePals (www.epals.com) is a safe, secure website to connect your students with a pen pal. You can search for other teachers who want to connect, and even narrow your search based on the topic you would like your students to discuss. Each student is provided with a digital pen pal that they write to using the secure website and email address provided by ePals. Teachers monitor the emails and must release emails after students have completed their drafts so that no email is sent without teacher approval. This is a wonderful method to allow students to connect with people in geographically and culturally different areas of the world to discuss ELA and social studies topics. Read more about promoting culture with social media in Figure 9.3.

Social media also provides unique opportunities to follow current news or cultural events. Although we like Twiducate for its secure educational platform, we believe Twitter is also useful for students to follow current events. Teachers can create a Twitter feed for the class to follow, without setting up personal accounts for students, that highlight events occurring that are relevant to classroom instruction. For example, during Black History Month, teachers can tweet (or post micro-blogs) about different cultural events happening in their cities or towns that students and parents might be interested in attending. Teachers can also tweet current event news stories

Textbox 9.1.

Focus On:
Promoting Cultural Understanding through Social Media

Challenge: Digital tools are a great way to bridge classrooms and expose students to other cultures and cultural influences through social media that connects to people in geographically different areas. However, it is sometimes difficult to know where to begin or set up a project that may do so.

Consider: Multiple digital tools offer ways for students to connect with and learn from students in other classrooms, cities, states, and even countries. Teachers may also use digital tools to connect with one another to set up learning opportunities between classrooms.

Tips:
1. Think about how you might integrate cultural activities within existing content (e.g., connecting students in different geographical regions during a geography unit).
2. Use a social network tool designed for education, such as ePals or Edmodo, to connect with teachers who may have the same interests as you to design and implement a unit that connects your students. You may also find teachers through professional networks.
3. Think about how you would like your students to interact with another class of students. For example, would you have them write one-on-one with a digital pen pal, or would you have students communicate in a whole-class video setting?
4. If you decide to have students engage in online discussion through discussion boards or electronic pen pals, consider if you will introduce classes via video tools, such as Skype, as this type of introduction may build rapport between students and promote excitement to participate in such a project.
5. Create cultural objectives along with instructional objectives to ensure students are engaging in cultural understanding in their social media projects.

Check Out: *Flat Classrooms Ning* (http://flatconnections.net/)

This social network site was created and designed for teachers to connect with other educators who want to engage their students in global connections. Multiple resources and connection tools are available through this site.

that they want students to access via tablets or laptops. Students can read the stories online and post their reactions on the teacher's class blog, which allows them to not only express their opinion but also read and react to other students' opinions.

Additionally, social media websites are available that allow teachers or students to conduct research on a current event topic and gather information. Sites such as Mashable (www.mashable.com) gather information from popular blog sites, Twitter, and new sites to compile information in a searchable platform. Students with more advanced research skills may find these types of sites useful for accessing multimedia resources on a current event topic. As these types of sites publish multiple types of videos and non-news affiliated users are allowed to upload videos, we recommend teachers at least do advance searches before students conduct multimedia research to view the type of content students will pull up.

SAMPLE LESSON

In the sample lesson in Table 9.1 students use Storify to curate information and create an informational narrative on a timely news topic. Storify is a free site that allows users to collect information from media across the web to create a comprehensive narrative on a topic. Users can gather information from multiple social media tools including, but not limited to, Twitter, Facebook, YouTube, Flickr, and Instagram. Users can then drag and drop tweets, status updates, photo, videos and more to bring together the social media elements that will best illustrate their story. Users can then create a narrative for all of the media elements by adding a headline, introduction, hyperlinks, and text anywhere it is needed to build a cohesive story and provide a context for readers.

ADDITIONAL RESOURCES FOR USING
SOCIAL MEDIA IN THE CLASSROOM

Table 9.2 presents a sampling of digital tools for integrating social media into the classroom. Consider how the grade level examples might be adapted for your classroom.

Table 9.1.   Fifth Grade Lesson Using Storify to Curate Information and Create an Informational Narrative on a News Topic

Instructional Goals of the Lesson: Students will use Storify to curate information and create a story and create an informational narrative on a timely news topic.

Common Core Standards Addressed:
CCSS.ELA-LITERACY.RI.5.4
Determine the meaning of general academic and domain-specific words and phrases in a text relevant to a *grade 5 topic or subject area.*
CCSS.ELA-LITERACY.RI.5.5
Compare and contrast the overall structure (e.g., chronology, comparison, cause/effect, problem/solution) of events, ideas, concepts, or information in two or more texts.
CCSS.ELA-LITERACY.RI.5.6
Analyze multiple accounts of the same event or topic, noting important similarities and differences in the point of view they represent.
CCSS.ELA-LITERACY.RI.5.7
Draw on information from multiple print or digital sources, demonstrating the ability to locate an answer to a question quickly or to solve a problem efficiently.
CCSS.ELA-LITERACY.RI.5.9
Integrate information from several texts on the same topic in order to write or speak about the subject knowledgeably.
CCSS.ELA-LITERACY.SL.5.2
Summarize a written text read aloud or information presented in diverse media and formats, including visually, quantitatively, and orally.

English Language Proficiency Standards Addressed:
1. Construct meaning from oral presentations and literary and informational text through grade-appropriate listening, reading, and viewing
3. Speak and write about grade-appropriate complex literary and informational texts and topics
1. Conduct research and evaluate and communicate findings to answer questions or solve problems
9. Create clear and coherent grade-appropriate speech and text

Lesson Description & Instructional Approach:
- The teacher should begin this lesson by describing a current news topic that is relevant to the grade level content being studied. For example, this could be a science or social studies topic, or even a topic about education, such as how students learn with technology.
- The teacher should then model how to use Storify to create an informational story. Although the tool is simple to use, the modeling should include how to search various social media outlets and add that information to a story. The teacher should also model how to add narrative text to create a meaningful informational story.
- The teacher should explain that students work should do the following:
  ○ Describe the meaning of specialized words related to the topic
  ○ Compare and contrast information from the various sources that they use
  ○ Integrate and summarize information from all of their sources to present their understanding and point of view on the topic

- Students should then begin creating their informational story. When finished, the story can be published to Storify and a link to the story can be shared through other social media.

See Figure 9.3 for an example of the Storify interface as a story is being created and Figure 9.4 for an example of a published Storify creation.

Digital Devices/Tools Used
- Computer or iPad
- Storify website (www.storify.com)

Digital Contribution to Instruction
- By using this digital curation tool, students gain experiences with the types of information presented through multiple social media outlets but only have to access a single site.
- Students get to use the most current information available on the topic by including information from social media sources that are constantly updated.
- Students get to user a wide variety of sources to illustrate their understanding.
- Students learn how various forms of media may contribute information on a topic.

Potential Constraints
- Although many of the social media outlets that can be accessed within the tool can be used without signing into an account, users must connect their accounts to integrate information from Twitter, Facebook and Instagram. **Potential Solution:** The teacher can create class accounts for each of these sites and instruct the students to connect with the class accounts rather than personal accounts. Additionally, the teacher may choose to not let students use information from one or more of these outlets.
- Students may have a difficult time selecting from so many resources or may choose so many resources that they may have difficulty synthesizing them or creating a narrative to go with the resources. **Potential Solution:** The teacher may limit the number of resources that students can include in their story.

Instructional Considerations
- The teacher should consider how this work will be evaluated. Considering the evaluation in advance will help the teacher provide clear expectations and instruction.
- The teacher should consider which social media outlets, if any, students will use to share their work through the share feature on the site.
- The teacher should consider if students' stories will be set as private or public.

Reflection
After conducting the lesson, consider the extent to which you were able to adhere to your instructional goal. What helped or hindered your students' abilities to meet the instructional goal? Note what you may need to do differently the next time you use these technologies.

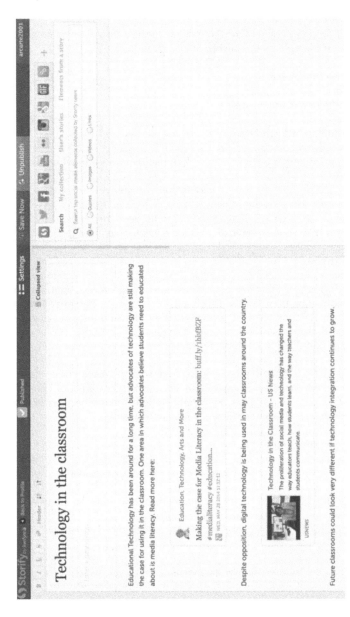

Figure 9.3. Example of Storify interface as a story is being created.

Technology in the classroom

arcarte2001 @arcarte2001

Published · Unpublished Edits · 0 total views

5 minutes ago · 0 total views

··· ▪▪ Template ☑ Share ☒ Edit

</> Embed

Educational Technology has been around for a long time, but advocates of technology are still making the case for using it in the classroom. One area in which advocates believe students need to educated about is media literacy. Read more here:

Education, Technology, Arts and More

Making the case for Media Literacy in the classroom: buff.ly/1hbfBZF #medialiteracy #education...
3 HOURS AGO

Despite opposition, digital technology is being used in may classrooms around the country.

Technology in the Classroom - US News

The proliferation of social media and technology has changed the way educators teach, how students learn, and the way teachers and students communicate.

Figure 9.4.   Example of a published Storify creation.

Table 9.2. Resources and Ideas for Integrating Social Media

Digital Resources	Possible Uses	Grade-Specific Examples & CCSS Addressed
Apps (Note: Apps are also available as an online resource): • Path • Pinterest • Instagram Online Resources: • Animoto (www.animoto.com) • Delicious (www.delicious.com) • Diigo (www.diigo.com) • Edmodo (www.edmodo.com) • ePals (www.epals.com) • Flickr (www.flickr.com) • Goodreads (www.goodreads.com) • Google + (www.plus.google.com) • My Big Campus (www.mybigcampus.com) • Ning (www.ning.com) • Tumblr (www.tumblr.com) • Twiducate (www.twiducate.com) • Twitter (www.twitter.com) • YouTube (www.youtube.com)	Students may: • Share ideas • Share photos and images • Build a repository of digital artifacts about a topic • Collaborate to create texts • Connect with audiences outside of the classroom • Employ questioning techniques • Role play • Engage in perspective taking • Annotate • Take and share notes • Follow current events or news • Summarize information • Bookmark websites Teachers may: • Provide notes • Inform students about assignments and class news • Connect with other classrooms • Engage students in research • Communicate with parents	**Kindergarten:** With guidance and support from a teacher, kindergarten students could create a class video about counting using Animoto and share the video with other classes and parents. **CCSS.ELA-Literacy.SL.K.4.** *Describe familiar people, places, things, and events and, with prompting and support, provide additional detail.* **CCSS.ELA-Literacy.SL.K.6.** *Speak audibly and express thoughts, feelings, and ideas clearly.* **First Grade:** As a class and with the help of a teacher, students can create a Pinterest board of images of items a fictional character may want or need based on events in a story or novel. **CCSS.ELA-Literacy.RL.1.3.** *Describe characters, settings, and major events in a story, using key details.* **Second Grade:** Students could post Tweets (or micro-blogs) in the perspective of a character from a fictional story.

Online resources for teacher development:
- Better Lesson (www.betterlesson.com)
- The Educator's PLN (www.edupln.ning .com)
- EduClipper (www.educlipper.net)
- Level Up Book Club (www.levelupbc. blogspot.ca)
- Professional Learning Practice (www .plpnetwork.com)
- Teach Ade (www.teachade.com)

- Network with other educators
- Share lesson plans
- Receive feedback on lessons and curricula

CCSS.ELA-Literacy.RL.2.6. *Acknowledge differences in the points of view of characters, including by speaking in a different voice for each character when reading dialogue aloud.*

Third Grade: Students may engage in a pen-pal project with a class in a different state to compare geographical features of their respective cities or towns.

CCSS.ELA-Literacy.W.3.6. *With guidance and support from adults, use technology to produce and publish writing (using keyboarding skills) as well as to interact and collaborate with others.*

Fourth Grade: Students could post and annotate online resources for a biography research project on a famous historical figure.

CCSS.ELA-Literacy.W.4.8. *Recall relevant information from experiences or gather relevant information from print and digital sources; take notes and categorize information, and provide a list of sources.*

Fifth Grade: With teacher supervision and parental permission, students may navigate book recommendations and post reactions to grade-level books read during independent reading.

(continued)

Table 9.2. (*continued*)

Digital Resources	Possible Uses	Grade-Specific Examples & CCSS Addressed
		CCSS.ELA-Literacy.RF.5.4.a. *Read grade-level text with purpose and understanding.* **CCSS.ELA-Literacy.W.5.1.** *Write opinion pieces on topics or texts, supporting a point of view with reasons and information.* **Sixth Grade:** Students could participate in online discussion using an education social network (e.g., Edmodo) to analyze a story or play read in English language arts. **CCSS.ELA-Literacy.RL.6.1.** *Cite textual evidence to support analysis of what the text says explicitly as well as inferences drawn from the text.* **CCSS.ELA-Literacy.W.6.1.** *Write arguments to support claims with clear reasons and relevant evidence.*

REFLECTION QUESTIONS

1. Although allowing students to use social media can seem daunting, there are many ways that social media can potentially support their learning. What are some of the ways that social media can support the literacy goals that you have for your students?
2. Explore some of the social media sites listed in this chapter. What Common Core State Standards could be addressed by having students participate in these sites?

REFERENCES

Colwell, J. (2012). Using a collaborative blog project to introduce disciplinary-literacy strategies in social studies pre-service teacher education. *Journal of School Connections, 4*(1), 25–52.

Hutchison, A., & Wang, W. (2012). Blogging within a social networking site as a form of literature response in a teacher education course. Educational Media International, 49(3). DOI:10.1080/09523987.2012.741197.

McGrail, E., & Davis, A. (2011). The influence of classroom blogging on elementary student writing. *Journal of Research in Childhood Education, 25*, 41–37.

Chapter Ten

The Flipped Classroom

Mrs. Johnson's students have become proficient with using many different digital devices and tools. She believes that she can make the most of their digital skills by instituting a flipped classroom model in which much of the primary instruction in her class takes place via online methods and class time is used for activities and group work. Although she is confident in her students' skills, she is still hesitant to flip her classroom because she has never seen a classroom using the flipped model and is not sure how it will work. She also knows that it will require extra time and energy on her part because, for her, it is a different way of teaching. However, after exploring more information on the topic, she believes that her students can benefit from this instructional model and she is ready to give it a try. Mrs. Johnson collaborates with her literacy coach to work through six steps (described subsequently in the section titled Steps for Flipping) recommended for adopting a flipped classroom model. She also works with the coach to consider how flipped instruction can address Common Core State Standards. After much preparation, Mrs. Johnson begins to gradually flip her classroom. Her students adapt well because of all the digital experience they have had throughout the year. She receives a lot of questions about the new approach, but she is able to provide reasons for her approach because she has considered it so carefully. Her approach is successful and she becomes a resource for other teachers in her school who want to try flipping their classrooms as well.

We discuss in this chapter the flipped classroom model, which is emerging as a popular method for blended instruction to incorporate digital tools in K-12 instruction. Although the flipped classroom is a method, rather than a type of digital tool, which we have previously focused on in this book, we consider this method useful as it may incorporate many of the tools we have already

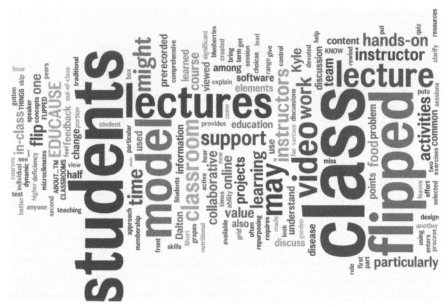

Figure 10.1.   Ideas related to the flipped classroom.

discussed in a different type of instruction. We present here the elements of a flipped classroom, how it might be appropriate for elementary grades, and things you may consider if you decide to try a flipped model in your instruction.

WHAT IS A FLIPPED CLASSROOM?

At the most basic level, flipping a classroom refers to positioning lecture as an out-of-class activity and homework as an in-class activity. Or, as Bergmann and Sams (2012) explain, "That which can be traditionally done in class is now done at home, and that which is traditionally done as homework is now completed in class" (p. 13). Essentially, flipping one's classroom involves creating lecture-based videos or digital presentations for students to view and learn from that would typically be a part of in-class instruction and then engaging students in reinforcement and practice activities in class that are traditionally reserved for homework. For example, students could watch a video about verbs and their purpose in grammar outside of the classroom and then practice using verbs in sentences, oral language activities, and identifying them in readings during class. The flipped model is promising because it places focus on students' practice with concepts and provides more time for teachers to work with students one-on-one or in small groups during class time. Although flipped classrooms are mostly seen at the high-school and college levels, because lecture is featured so prominently at those levels, resources have begun to appear for elementary teachers to flip their classrooms and instruction. Flipped classroom models are relatively new to the K-12 sector, so research is still emerging that speaks to various aspects of a flipped model. However, many online resources, published through education organizations or online platforms, are available for teachers to use when flipping their classrooms. One resource that discusses the flipped elementary classroom and provides links to various online sites devoted to the topic that we found useful was through the *Reading Rockets* website (see www.reading rockets.org/blog/55627).

LEARNING POSSIBILITIES

The flipped classroom model holds potential for student learning as students are able to spend more time activating and practicing skills during class time than they would in a more teacher-centered learning environment. Students are able to spend as much time as they need watching, pausing, or rewinding videos to better understand lecture material. Thus, students who struggle to keep up with notes, who miss class, or who sometimes need more time to understand teacher lecture may remain more actively engaged in the learning process (Bergmann & Sams, 2012). The learning process is thus self-paced. Students must also learn to ask questions and self-check their learning as they watch the videos, which begin to lay foundations for activating students' critical thinking skills and also supports study and comprehension skills.

After students have moved through the video lessons at their own pace, they engage in collaborative and student-driven activity, creating an engaging learning environment. Teachers may incorporate small-group learning activities to produce materials or to apply learning to practice to test and extend students' understanding of the video material. Students who struggle with learning may also be provided more individual support with this model as the teacher has more opportunities to focus on individual student learning because less class time is taken up with lecture. As Bretzmann (2013) suggests, the flipped classroom forces the teacher-student relationship to change. Students and teachers must collaborate with students and help them take charge of their learning. You may also find that you develop closer learning relationships with your students and learn more about them as you collaborate in class. Additionally, by having your students learn with technology at home, you bring parents in on the action and provide them with a closer look at the topics their children are studying.

CAN I FLIP AN ELEMENTARY CLASSROOM?

At this point you may be thinking, "Ok, this sounds interesting (and different!), but how can this model work with my young students who have problems staying on task or are just learning how to interact in a classroom setting?" Like you, we also had our concerns about a flipped classroom model in grades prior to middle and high school. However, we adopted the perspective that a flipped classroom in K-6 does not necessarily have to look like a flipped classroom in the middle and upper grades. Principles from the flipped model can still be applied to achieve similar learning objectives even if you do not have your second graders watch a thirty-minute lecture on Native Americans for homework. (In fact, we strongly discourage you from doing so.)

Instead, consider aspects of a particular lesson that you might flip. Going back to the Native American topic example, consider a lesson you might implement to help your students learn about various Native American tribes and their characteristics. What aspects of that lesson would be best suited for flipping? Often, at the elementary level, background information is well-suited for flipping during a lesson. Perhaps you have a five-minute video about characteristics of different Native American tribes that students could view at a station and take notes on using a note guide or respond to via some type of writing assignment, digital or traditional. Or, you may consider making a short video or narrated presentation with images to provide your students with background information. In other words, reconsider how video is sometimes used in a lesson or unit to provide reinforcement, and create learning opportunities by building students' prior knowledge with digital video or images so that they may engage in practice activities to extend their learning. Jon Bergmann (2012), an educator who uses and writes about the flipped classroom model, suggests useful tips for elementary teachers, such as keeping videos ten minutes or shorter, determining ahead of time how students will access videos, and considering how you will assess that the students watched the video (for the full list visit http://jonbergmann.com/flipping-the-elementary-classroom).

STEPS FOR FLIPPING

If you think that a flipped classroom model might be a welcome change to your current instruction, we outline here steps to take to best adapt this model for your classroom.

1. Think about the scale of flipping that you want to implement. Although little research currently exists for the flipped classroom model at the elementary level, many teachers have implemented and blogged or written about their flipped classrooms. Most, such as Todd Nesloney (2013), recommend starting small with no more than two or three flipped lessons per week. Once you and your students become more comfortable with the model, you may want to include more flipped lessons in your planning, as long as you feel and your assessments indicate that students are learning with this model.

2. You may want to explain what flipping is to upper elementary students who are more familiar with traditional models of classroom instruction so that they will understand why their classwork looks different from previous classes or years in school.

3. Decide on the digital platform you will use to host your videos or lessons that you post online for students to view outside of class or in stations. Many of the social networks, such as Edmodo, that we have already discussed in this book are excellent and safe platforms for hosting videos and artifacts that students can easily access. Another platform created specifically for the flipped classroom method is Sophia (www.sophia .org). Sophia allows teachers to set up a free account, create a class group that they can manage and only their students can access, search for videos that other teachers have posted (or create and post their own), and assess students' learning with digital tools built into the platform. The platform also hosts screencasting tools for teachers to use to build short (fifteen-minutes or less) videos to guide students through PowerPoint presentations, PDF handouts, or images that will connect directly to their accounts. Essentially, teachers create tutorials through Sophia that students simply visit and complete. Teachers should also include assessment tools, such as Google forms, for the student to complete after viewing the material in the tutorial to track students' learning about the topic.

4. Spend ample time instructing your students in using the digital platform. Complete a few sample tutorials or videos together so that they become comfortable with using the technology.

5. After students have watched videos or lessons or completed tutorials, read through or grade the assessments to determine where students struggled, or were most actively engaged, during the online work. This information allows teachers to provide individual attention, catered to specific needs, to students during the class activities that will follow the online activities.

6. Decide on the type of in-class activities that students will engage in after viewing the online materials. Project-based learning that allows students

to build or create products that reflect their learning gives teachers the opportunity to walk around the classroom and individually assist students. Further, when students are asked to create products based on the knowledge they gained from the online tutorials or videos, teachers can more accurately gauge students' understanding of a topic or lesson. This process may encourage students to become more reflective than when they take a traditional test or quiz, and teachers who have flipped their classrooms report students' scores on assessments increased due to the flipped structure of instruction that allows for individual student pacing and hands-on, highly-reflective follow-up practice (Bergmann & Sams, 2012).

CONNECTING A FLIPPED MODEL TO THE CCSS

The type of learning that a flipped classroom promotes can readily be connected to the Common Core State Standards to promote students literacy skills in K-6 education. We address the anchor standards to examine these connections.

Reading

Students are required to use reading and thinking skills when they watch videos or view digital tutorials for homework or at independent classroom stations. Thus, they are evaluating content in diverse media and formats (CCSS.ELA-Literacy.CCRA.R.7). Students must also understand and evaluate arguments and information that the videos are presenting to comprehend the content of the videos (CCSS.ELA-Literacy.CCRA.R.8). The videos will also present central ideas, and students must be able to summarize these ideas to show their understanding of the videos (CCSS.ELA-Literacy.CCRA.R.2). Further, videos often present more complex ideas and text to build background knowledge and can do so in a manner that students better understand than reading a written text, particularly at a young age. The flipped classroom method encourages the independent comprehension of informational videos (see CCSS.ELA-Literacy.CCRA.R.10). Finally, when students engage in classroom activity using the knowledge they learned from the videos or tutorials they must be able to use evidence to support conclusions drawn from the video (text) in their writing or speaking (CCSS.ELA-Literacy.CCRA.R.1).

Writing

Because the flipped classroom method involves students viewing videos or tutorials, completing assessments, and completing in-class activities to extend and practice the knowledge learned during the videos, multiple areas of writing can be targeted. Teachers can have students write informative or explanatory texts to analyze the content of the videos (CCSS.ELA-Literacy. CCRA.W.2) as a quick assessment following viewing, or have students produce much longer or detailed texts during in-class activity to show their understanding. You may also incorporate digital tools into the tutorials as assessments, such as Google forms, which allow students to publish writing using technology, or Edmodo discussion boards, to help them interact with other students (CCSS.ELA-Literacy.CCRA.W.6). Because the videos in flipped classrooms are often watched outside of class or during independent work, a flipped classroom model may be an excellent way to have students complete research projects. Students can watch tutorials on how to gather relevant sources and then spend class time actually gathering sources and evaluating the credibility of the sources (CCSS.ELA-Literacy.CCRA.W.8) with individual assistance from the teacher. The videos can also serve as informational text that students draw evidence from to support analysis, reflection, and research (CCSS.ELA-Literacy.CCRA.W.9).

Speaking and Listening

The flipped classroom model provides ample class time for collaboration and student interaction as they complete projects and assignments to reflect on their learning from videos. Teachers can pair students to help them complete projects that require students to converse and build on each other's ideas (CCSS.ELA-Literacy.CCRA.SL.1). Students must again use the knowledge they gained from the videos to integrate and evaluation information with which they were presented in visual and oral format (CCSS.ELA-Literacy. CCRA.SL.2). These conversations will help build students' oral language skills so that they demonstrate command of formal English (CCSS.ELA-Literacy.CCRA.SL.6).

TIPS FOR FLIPPING

Here are a few suggestions to help you get started flipping your classroom:

- Read as much as you can on the subject. Like we said before, little research currently exists for the flipped model. However, many websites and blogs have been devoted to using this model, and we recommend visiting those sites. Particularly, you may want to visit the sites of a few universities that have explanations of the flipped classroom method on their education

webpages. We found Vanderbilt University's website (http://cft.vanderbilt
.edu/guides-sub-pages/flipping-the-classroom/) and University of Texas
at Austin's site (http://ctl.utexas.edu/teaching/flipping_a_class/what_is
_flipped) helpful in their descriptions of the flipped classroom and its ori-
gin. These sites also offer connections to theory that are particularly useful for educators. Another useful place to find information is through the
Flipped Learning Network's Ning (http://flippedclassroom.org), which is
a professional development forum that allows educators to come together
in a social network to discuss flipped classrooms, post videos showcasing
their flipped classrooms, and post and answer inquiries about flipping a
classroom. This organization also has a webpage that offers resources to
use in a flipped classroom (see www.flippedlearning.org).

- Visit Twitter to search and find teachers and other professional development organizations who post and write about flipped classrooms. Just typing in "flipped classroom" yields multiple sites to visit and find resources.
- Find another teacher at your school or one who teaches in your grade level
  who is also interested in the flipped classroom model. You can support
  one another as you flip your classroom or lessons and share resources you
  might create.
- Provide parents with literature on or a presentation about the flipped classroom at an open house or orientation. Let parents know your reasons for
  introducing a flipped model in your classroom and how this model can
  support their child's learning.
- Solicit feedback from parents. If you assign videos or tutorials for homework, parents will play a critical role in helping their children play or access
  these learning tools. Ask parents how they view this process and offer them
  a chance to describe the advantages and disadvantages of this model in regard to their child. Doing so will reinforce collaboration between you and
  your students' parents, and give you insight into how the tools you have
  selected are performing in a child's home.
- Solicit feedback from students. Give them opportunities to tell you what is
  or is not working for them with the flipped classroom. You could make this
  feedback a writing assignment using a digital tool, which would promote
  literacy skills while also giving you a chance to learn about your students'
  opinions.

AN EXAMPLE OF A FLIPPED LESSON

We conclude this chapter by presenting a narrative describing the way that
one elementary teacher, Ms. Martinez, incorporated a flipped classroom ap-

proach into her second grade curriculum. Our intent is for this narrative to provide ideas to consider when flipping your classroom or a lesson.

Context

Ms. Martinez is a second-grade teacher at an elementary school in a large, urban area of the United States. The school is located in a state that has adopted the Common Core State Standards, and she is required to align her instruction with these standards. Recently, Ms. Martinez has become disheartened because many students in her class received low test scores on a state standardized test to measure English Language Arts (ELA) skills. She has tried multiple methods of instruction to help improve her students' ELA skills but finds intervention difficult because of the different reading ability levels represented in her classroom. For example, out of twenty students, fifteen read below grade level, three read on grade level, and two above grade level. Ms. Martinez is also concerned because the CCSS require her students to use analysis skills that are often associated with higher-order thinking, and the fifteen students who read below grade level struggle to engage in analysis. Also, the fifteen struggling readers are diverse in the areas of reading in which they struggle. For example, some struggle with fluency, some with decoding, and some with both.

Considering a Flipped Classroom Approach

Another teacher, Ms. Frank, who is also a second-grade teacher at Ms. Martinez's school suggests a flipped classroom approach to instruction. Ms. Frank explains that she has had success with this approach, although she has only used it for a few lessons, and encourages Ms. Martinez to try it in her own classroom. Ms. Martinez becomes interested in a flipped method of instruction because of Ms. Frank's descriptions about how the video tutorials provided added support for her struggling readers. Ms. Frank explained that she created videos of screencasts of her reading online stories aloud, with pause-and-reflect moments added into the reading, and a quick exit ticket assessment using a Google form for her students to summarize the story. After providing Ms. Martinez with multiple resources to read and consider the approach, Ms. Frank offered to share her videos with Ms. Martinez and also shows Ms. Martinez a tutorial on YouTube for creating a screencast if she decides to make her own video.

Planning

Because Ms. Martinez's school district uses Edmodo as a digital learning platform, she knows that sixteen of her students have computers at home, with twelve of those computers connected to the Internet. However, all of her students' parents have smart phones with the Edmodo app downloaded, so she feels comfortable having students watch a video at home. Ms. Martinez decides to first flip a lesson on a short fiction story to have her students watch a video of a read-aloud at home and engage in writing a story with a similar structure and main idea during in-class activity.

Ms. Martinez liked Ms. Frank's screencast idea, but does not yet feel comfortable with screencast technology and creating her own screencast. She decides to instead video record herself reading a hardback fiction book (with the camera focused on the book pages), using her finger to follow along as she reads, and stopping to ask questions as she reads. Because this will be her first time using a flipped approach, and because some of her students will probably watch the video on their parents' smart phone, she provides a fillable worksheet for her students to respond to the questions she poses as she is reading in the video. Some of these questions align with plot-based elements of the story, some with thematic elements of the story, and some with structural aspects of the story. She also rarely asks students to work on Edmodo at home, so she does not want to overwhelm her students with too many assignments with digital technology at once. Ms. Martinez also decides to allow any student who cannot access the video outside of class to watch it on the classroom computer during independent reading time or before or after school.

Ms. Martinez plans to have students use the fillable worksheets for reference during their story-writing activity in class. During that part of class, she will organize desks into clusters so that she can provide individual attention to students while also allowing students to work together. She decides to have students outline their stories on paper, and then she will build on this activity in another lesson so that students can create and illustrate their stories using the StoryMaker app on the school's iPads. Read more about planning for flipped instruction in Textbox 10.1.

Standards

To ensure that her lesson addresses the standards she has targeted, Ms. Martinez uses a table to chart standards to learning activities in the lesson (see Table 10.1).

Summary

Although Ms. Martinez's flipped classroom was really a flipped lesson, she still provided a fresh approach to help her struggling readers understand a story

---

Textbox 10.1.

Focus On:
Preparing Students for a Flipped Classroom

Challenge: This chapter provided a breakdown of how to flip the elementary classroom. As discussed, this process may be confusing to students as it represents a different type of learning than most have previously experienced.

Consider: We present here a summary of tips and things to think about as you prepare to flip your classroom.

Tips:
1. Flip a lesson, not an entire class at the elementary level.
2. Explain to students why you are flipping your lesson and how they can benefit from the lesson.
3. Explain to parents why you are flipping your lesson and how they can help their children best engage in their digital homework.
4. Spend multiple class sessions allowing students to become accustomed to using the technology they will be using to complete homework assignments.
5. Set aside time before each activity-driven portion of the flipped class for students to ask questions they may have had during the digital, independent portion of the lesson.

Check Out: *The Flipped Learning Network* (http://flippedlearning.org/FLN)

This site is devoted to flipping classrooms and lessons and provides multiple resources for teachers to view and consider as they begin preparations to flip their classrooms.

---

and then engage in their own writing to reflect on their learning. Her lesson incorporated traditional and digital types of reading and writing, and provided opportunities for independent, collaborative, and teacher-supported learning. Finally, her flipped lesson addressed multiple objectives of the CCSS.

CLOSING THOUGHTS

Although the flipped classroom model is relatively new, we expect to see research and more formal writing on it appear in the next few years. It has created a buzz among many teachers, both in higher levels of education and K-12. We think the model holds promise for reaching multiple types

Table 10.1.   CCSS Addressed with the Flipped Lesson

Lesson task	*CCSS Addressed*
Have students read a short story to understand and respond to questions about plot, thematic, and structural elements of fiction.	CCSS.ELA-Literacy.RL.2.1 Ask and answer such questions as *who, what, where, when, why,* and *how* to demonstrate understanding of key details in a text. CCSS.ELA-Literacy.RL.2.5 Describe the overall structure of a story, including describing how the beginning introduces the story and the ending concludes the action. CCSS.ELA-Literacy.RL.2.7 Use information gained from the illustrations and words in a print or digital text to demonstrate understanding of its characters, setting, or plot.
Have students listen to the story while they watch and follow along with the teacher.	CCSS.ELA-Literacy.SL.2.2 Recount or describe key ideas or details from a text read aloud or information presented orally or through other media. CCSS.ELA-Literacy.SL.2.3 Ask and answer questions about what a speaker says in order to clarify comprehension, gather additional information, or deepen understanding of a topic or issue.
Have students work together to write a story.	CCSS.ELA-Literacy.W.2.6 With guidance and support from adults, use a variety of digital tools to produce and publish writing, including in collaboration with peers. CCSS.ELA-Literacy.SL.2.1 Participate in collaborative conversations with diverse partners about *grade 2 topics and texts* with peers and adults in small and larger groups.
Have students compose an original story that uses similar plot, thematic and structural elements of the story read in the video.	CCSS.ELA-Literacy.W.2.3 Write narratives in which they recount a well-elaborated event or short sequence of events, include details to describe actions, thoughts, and feelings, use temporal words to signal event order, and provide a sense of closure. CCSS.ELA-Literacy.W.2.6 With guidance and support from adults, use a variety of digital tools to produce and publish writing, including in collaboration with peers.

of learners and in more seamlessly incorporating technology into classroom learning in a manner that actively engages students and parents. We hope that you consider the ideas in this chapter as you think about how a flipped classroom may work in your own teaching.

REFLECTION QUESTIONS

1. What are some of the potential barriers to flipping your classroom? Brainstorm a list of possible solutions for these barriers and determine if flipping might be right for your classroom.
2. View this infographic on the flipped classroom: www.knewton.com/flipped-classroom/. Does flipping seem like a good idea for your classroom? How can you collaborate with another teacher to share the work required to flip your classroom?

Chapter Eleven

Managing the Digital Classroom

As we have described throughout this book, many new considerations must be taken into account when digital technology is integrated into the classroom. Some aspects of teaching with digital technology that require special consideration include how students will submit and share digital work, with whom the work will be shared given the ease of sharing work through social media, how the work will be evaluated, and how the work will be stored and accessed. It is also important to consider how students' understanding can be monitored when they work in digital spaces. This chapter is focused on these topics.

SUBMITTING DIGITAL WORK

Determining how your students will submit digital assignments can be a challenge. One reason is that students may be using tablets, and some tablet-based apps have limited ways to share work. Some of the ways that tablet apps allow users to share work are by emailing a link to the product, by posting a link to a social media site such as Facebook or Twitter, by uploading videos to YouTube, or by saving work to a cloud-based storage system such as Dropbox. Although these options are provided, teachers may not wish for students to share their work so publicly. Further, not all apps have such sophisticated options. There are several options that can make digital assignments more manageable. We describe a few of these options in the subsequent sections.

Screen Shots

A simple option for many digital products that students create is to have them take a screen shot of the work, which will save it to the camera roll on an iPad or to a file on some other tablets. Different tablets require different procedures for taking screen shots. On an iPad, a screen shot can be taken by simultaneously pressing the home and power buttons. Once the screen shot is saved to the camera roll, the work can be emailed. This method works well for assignments where the work appears on a single screen, such as a digital drawing or even for an app such as Magnetic Alphabet HD where students are spelling words on the screen.

Cloud-based Storage Systems

Another helpful option for collecting digital work is to have students save the work to a cloud-based storage system such as Dropbox. With tools like Dropbox, the user can save virtually any type of file, including photos and videos, and then share a link to the file so that anyone with the link can view it. Users can also create shared folders, which allow anyone who is invited to the shared digital folder to save work to the folder. All users will be able to see all files in the shared folders. This is a good option for classrooms because each student can have a shared folder with the teacher. All of the students' work can be submitted to their shared folders and collected throughout the year, essentially creating a digital portfolio of each student's work.

These types of storage systems are also particularly helpful because they can be accessed across multiple devices. For example, files in a Dropbox folder can be accessed through an app on an iPad or iPhone, or from any web-enabled device by going to the Dropbox website (www.dropbox.com). This feature allows students to access their work from anywhere so that they can continue work outside of school. It also allows teachers to access the work from anywhere so that they can evaluate student products without having to print or download them. One of the most helpful features of Dropbox is that it is integrated with many tablet-based apps. Therefore, students can access work that is saved in Dropbox from many apps, or easily save the work that they create in an app to Dropbox.

A similar tool that was created specifically for classrooms is Penzu Classroom. This cloud-based tool allows teachers to set up passcode-protected classroom accounts where students can submit assignments to the teacher. The teacher can make comments to the student on any portion of the text through an in-line commenting feature and grade the work. Students receive a notification that the teacher has provided comments or a grade. Perhaps one of the most useful features of Penzu Classroom is that teachers can create and send assignments to students. This feature is helpful because teachers can use it to provide guidelines and rubrics to students so that the students can easily reference them without having to have instructions printed on a piece of paper.

Video Storage Systems

In addition to cloud-based storage systems for documents, presentations, and photos, there are cloud-based storage systems specifically designed for storing videos. These types of storage systems are helpful and necessary because video files are often too large to share through email or require too much space to store in other systems such as Dropbox. A popular site for storing video files is Vimeo (www.vimeo.com), which we discussed in a previous chapter. This site works well for work created on tablets because Vimeo is integrated with many apps, allowing the user to upload a video directly from the app to Vimeo. Similarly, the iPad allows videos from the camera roll to be uploaded directly to Vimeo or YouTube. Vimeo is a password-protected site, so student work can be stored safely and can only be viewed when access is provided.

Another way to share videos is to upload them to YouTube. Although YouTube videos can be publicly shared, they can also be set to private or as unlisted, meaning that only users who are provided with the link can view the videos. This option also works well because YouTube is a free site and is also integrated into many apps, making it simple to export work that is created on a tablet such as the iPad. Another helpful feature of YouTube is that students can record a video directly to YouTube from the built-in camera on a computer or tablet.

Course Management Systems

Another option for managing students' digital work is through the use of a course management system. A course management system is a collection of tools that provide an online environment for course interactions. There are many free and paid course management systems that allow teachers to post assignments and files, host online discussions, send reminders and more. These tools also allow students to submit digital work through the course management system website. One example of this type of site is Edmodo (www.edmodo.com). Edmodo is a social platform that looks and feels similar to Facebook, but was created with schools in mind. It provides a space for students to collaborate and have discussions online and to submit assignments. Other examples include Schoolbinder (www.myschoolbinder.com) and Collaborize Classroom (www.collaborizeclassroom.com). Although these sites have many features that can facilitate instruction, the ability for students to submit digital work is a highlight of these tools. We discuss in Figure 11.1 how course management websites are commonly being used during substitute instruction and snow days to keep students and curriculum on track.

Textbox 11.1.

Focus On:
Using Course Management to Substitute Class

Challenge: Unexpected absences from work, inclement weather cancellation days, and substitute teachers who do not always follow the lesson plans we provide can easily derail a unit and make it difficult to keep on track with long-range planning. Additionally, sometimes students must miss multiple days of school due to illness and other issues, and often these students fall behind even if they are given homework ahead of time.

Consider: Course management sites (CMS) specifically designed for K-12 education, such as Edmodo, may be a useful tool to engage your students in active learning during your or their absence from school.

Tips:
1. Post videos of lessons on a CMS so that students can watch and listen to you to learn material. Additionally, parents can view these lessons to provide additional support for students.
2. Create small group discussions on a CMS where students can discuss material with one another via discussion board postings.
3. Post assignments, readings, and other lesson materials on a CMS for parents to view and work with students during absences from school.
4. Create an interactive lesson for students that incorporates various types of digital tools that support video, audio, written, and oral components to support multiple learning styles.
5. Include assessments in the form of written or oral responses to consider what students have learned during their online class and where you should begin with instruction when you next meet face-to-face.

Check Out: *CourseSites* by Blackboard (www.coursesites.com)

CourseSites is an educational CMS that offers many useful tools such as quiz creators, forums for discussion, and a grade center. This site also allows teachers to divide their courses into subjects, which is particularly useful at the elementary level if teachers use this site to engage their students in learning during an inclement weather cancellation day or during a day the teacher must be absent from school.

USING TECHNOLOGY TO FACILITATE
COMMUNICATION AND MONITOR UNDERSTANDING

Digital technology can be a wonderful tool for facilitating communication with students and their parents, as well as monitoring students' understanding of concepts that are presented in the classroom. A tool that we like for communicating with students and their parents is Remind 101. This tool provides an easy way for teachers to send mass text messages to students and parents without invading their privacy. Teachers can use Remind101 to send text message reminders and notification to students and parents about upcoming tests, homework assignments, due dates, and events.

In addition to this type of communication, many digital tools that have been discussed in this book have simple, built-in ways to share digital work. We highly recommend that you share students' digital work with parents in this way. Beschorner & Hutchison (2013) found that even in preschool, students were able to learn how to e-mail their digital work to their parents. The children's parents were delighted to receive the work and have a better sense of the kind of instruction happening in the classroom. Further, parents may enjoy following a class Twitter page or blog to stay updated on their children's work and learn ways to support their children at home.

There are also many ways to monitor students' understanding through digital tools. Two of the tools we have seen used most effectively in the classroom are Socrative (www.socrative.com) and Poll Everywhere (www .polleverywhere.com). Socrative can be accessed from computers, tablets, or smartphones and allows teachers to quickly create and send real-time formative assessment questions for students to respond to through a multiple-choice, true or false, or short-answer format. Students' responses are then available to the teacher in an Excel file or can be accessed online through a Google spreadsheet. Socrative also allows teachers to create quizzes, games, and exit tickets. Teachers can use the exit ticket feature to require students to answer a quick question before they leave class in order to gain feedback that can help shape the instruction for the next day.

Similar to Socrative, Poll Everywhere can be used to ask a question or solicit comments on a topic. Students can respond using Twitter, smart phones, or a web browser. Results can be projected live as responses are submitted. Another way to use this tool in a classroom could be as a method for students to ask questions as they work on group projects. If students are working in groups around the room, the teacher may be engaged with one group while the other groups work independently and may thus be unavailable to answer questions. The teacher could project the Poll Everywhere site on a screen and students could submit any questions or comments they have to Poll Everywhere as they work. As the questions and comments come up on the screen, other students in the class can attempt to answer the questions, or the teacher can be alerted that there is a question that needs to be addressed. This is only one suggestion of the many ways that this versatile tool can be used to engage students and monitor their understanding. Other tools with similar functions that teachers may wish to use are ClassPager (www.classpager.com), GoSoapBox (www.gosoapbox.com), and Mentimeter (www.mentimeter.com).

One other way to engage students and monitor their understanding is through a backchannel. A backchannel is facilitated through an online site, and provides a place for listeners to ask each other questions, provide comments, or request more information on a topic. Backchannels are used to hold a real-time conversation online alongside a speaker or presenter. In the classroom, a backchannel could be used when there is a guest speaker, when watching a video, or when students are working on the same topic independently or in small groups. A popular site used for creating a backchannel is TodaysMeet (www.todaysmeet.com). This site allows the user to create a "room" where the conversation can take place online, and to specify how long the room remains open.

EVALUATING DIGITAL WORK

Understanding how to evaluate work that students do online or create with digital tools is a common challenge for literacy teachers (Hutchison & Reinking, 2011). Teachers must not only consider how they will evaluate the print-based literacy skills that an activity addresses, but also the digital literacy skills involved. Further, teachers must decide how to determine students' understanding from a digital product that typically does not involve right and wrong answers. One of the first considerations for assessing digital work is to determine the skills, both digital and non-digital, that are addressed and developed through the work. In regard to the digital literacy skills addressed, there are many digital literacy skills built into the Common Core English Language Arts Standards. These skills can be grouped into five major areas, which are listed and described in Table 11.1. The digital literacy skills listed in this table are loosely based on Eshet-Alkalai's (2004) conceptual model for digital literacy, but have been updated to reflect current technologies and to align with the Common Core State Standards.

The digital literacy skills listed in Table 11.1 are important for students to acquire in order to best utilize and learn with digital technology. Therefore, these skills can serve as a starting point for assigning and evaluating students'

Table 11.1.   Digital Literacy Skills and Their Connections to the Common Core State Standards

Type of Digital Literacy	Description	Connection to Common Core State Standards
Multimodal understanding	This literacy refers to students' abilities to understand and evaluate information that is presented through any combination of text, visual, and audio resources, such as photos, illustrations, icons, videos, podcasts, and music.	CCSS.ELA-Literacy.CCRA.R.7 Integrate and evaluate content presented in diverse media and formats, including visually and quantitatively, as well as in words. CCSS.ELA-Literacy.CCRA.SL.2 Integrate and evaluate information presented in diverse media and formats, including visually, quantitatively, and orally.
Production of multimodal text	This literacy refers to students' abilities to produce information that combines text, visual, and audio resources to effectively convey meaning and enhance understanding of their ideas.	CCSS.ELA-Literacy.CCRA.SL.5 Make strategic use of digital media and visual displays of data to express information and enhance understanding of presentations. CCSS.ELA-Literacy.CCRA.R.7 Integrate and evaluate content presented in diverse media and formats, including visually and quantitatively, as well as in words. CCSS.ELA-Literacy.CCRA.SL.2 Integrate and evaluate information presented in diverse media and formats, including visually, quantitatively, and orally.
Digital navigation and synthesis	This literacy refers to students' abilities to navigate online text, including hyperlinks and multiple websites, to toggle between multiple applications and websites, to synthesize and make meaning from information gained from multiple online sources, and to communicate information gathered from multiple online sources.	CCSS.ELA-Literacy.CCRA.W.8 Gather relevant information from multiple print and digital sources, assess the credibility and accuracy of each source, and integrate the information while avoiding plagiarism.

(continued)

Table 11.1. (*continued*)

Type of Digital Literacy	Description	Connection to Common Core State Standards
Evaluation of online sources	This literacy refers to students' abilities to evaluate the validity and reliability of information and to identify false, irrelevant, or biased information.	CCSS.ELA-Literacy.CCRA.W.8 Gather relevant information from multiple print and digital sources, assess the credibility and accuracy of each source, and integrate the information while avoiding plagiarism.
Digital collaboration and participation skills	This literacy refers to students' abilities to understand the norms of participation and collaboration in online knowledge communities, discussion groups, and social media sites, as well as their abilities to discern what information should and should not be communicated in these public spaces.	CCSS.ELA-Literacy.CCRA.W.6 Use technology, including the Internet, to produce and publish writing and to interact and collaborate with others

digital work. However, there are many additional considerations for digital work as well. The manner in which digital work is evaluated will vary from tool to tool. For example, videos will be evaluated differently than blog posts, because videos are typically more image-based and blogs are typically more text-based. However, both can be used to assess understanding. Some general guidelines for assessing digital work are provided in figure 11.1. These guidelines are adapted from those created for instructors at the University of Wisconsin (http://engage.wisc.edu/dma/resources/grading.php).

Regardless of the assignment, the most important consideration for digital assignments is to set clear expectations for the students and to provide clear guidelines regarding how the work will be evaluated. This approach will require teachers to carefully consider in advance how they will evaluate students' work. Some examples of rubrics used for evaluating digital work can be found at this site: www.schrockguide.net/assessment-and-rubrics.html. Once guidelines are established, a digital rubric can easily be created and shared with students so that they can access the rubric as they work. With clear evaluation guidelines established in advance, both teachers and students will better know how to approach the digital work and will know what skills students should gain from the work.

Literacy Skills
- Identify the digital and non-digital literacy skills that are addressed and developed through the digital media assignment.

Type of grade
- If applicable, determine whether students will receive a group grade, individual grades, or a combination of the two.

Effectiveness
- Consider ways to assess projects on the following: clarity of ideas and details, overall organization, effective use of language, voice and audience, and technical competence.

Phases
- Identify logical phases for the development of the assignment (i.e., storyboarding, script writing, rough draft, critique and feedback, and final due date).

Formative feedback
- Provide feedback for projects at each phase of the assignment.

Media Quality
- Evaluate the quality of the resulting media by reviewing items such as length, pacing, appropriate use of transitions, and video quality.

Figure 11.1.   Guidelines for evaluating digital media assignments.

REFLECTION QUESTIONS

1. What is the most difficult aspect of managing your digital classroom? Talk to an instructional leader and colleague to come up with some strategies for approaching your digital classroom management challenges.
2. Explore the rubrics for evaluating digital work that can be found at this site: www.schrockguide.net/assessment-and-rubrics.html. How can you use these rubrics to help you develop your own ways of evaluating your students' digital work?

REFERENCES

Beschorner, B., & Hutchison, A. (2013a). iPads as tools for communicating with parents. *The Oklahoma Reader*, 49(1), 17–19.

Hutchison, A., & Reinking, D. (2011). Teachers' perceptions of integrating information and communication technologies into literacy instruction: A national survey in the U.S. *Reading Research Quarterly, 46*(4), 308–29.

Chapter Twelve

Issues Relevant to Using Digital Tools in the K-6 Classroom

We know that although digital technology may enhance instruction, there are many considerations for incorporating digital tools and resources into the classroom. This chapter provides an overview of issues or obstacles that may arise when using digital technology and presents possible solutions or resources to visit to guide you in planning.

DIGITAL COPYRIGHT

We begin by looking at copyright issues and copyright law, which carry some of the most serious consequences for misuse of digital technology. Copyright is also a legal area that has changed drastically with the advent of digital technology and public distribution of resources and ideas on the Internet. As a teacher, you are well accustomed to dealing with copyright with print-based materials, but how familiar are you with copyright of digital resources? Copyright exists to protect authors and to prohibit personal gain from another person's ideas. Although personal gain is indeed rare in the K-12 education domain, what can we do as teachers to protect another person's work and model for our students how to appropriately use digital technology?

Within the realm of teaching and education, arguably one of the most important aspects of copyright to attend to when planning technology-based or driven instruction is fair use and the consideration of whether the copy, distribution, or use of authored material is reasonable. Although much Internet-based digital material exists in public domain or through educational websites for public use, some digital resources, such as films, art, and music, have copyrights. When using copyright materials fair use must be considered. Broadly, we must think about personal and financial gain based on reproduction or distribution of web resources, the type of digital work that we are distributing to our students, how much of that work we are distributing, and how the use of the digital materials will affect the author's ability to profit from the work. For a detailed overview of fair use, please visit the U.S. Copyright Office's website, http://www.copyright.gov/fls/fl102.html.

Software copyright is also important to understand. Although software is usually purchased and manually installed on computers, it is still a digital resource with copyright. Be sure to read the software company's policy on copyright, including how many computers the software can be installed on and policy on how to copy software for back-up use. Most licenses will allow the copying of software to serve as back-up if the original program is damaged or destroyed, but few will allow multiple installations of a software program unless individual licenses are purchased for each computer. When in doubt, just contact the software representative if you are struggling with how to legally install or use your classroom software.

For most of the classroom activities we engage our students in using digital tools, students will only need to cite the digital resource if they use it for a project or to publish to a personal blog. Additionally, if you as the teacher are posting useful web-based information on your blog site, it is fair to publish a link to the information rather than copying and pasting the information online on your personal site. However, be sure to carefully study web resources before using them to look for guidelines on copyright and how materials may be distributed in your classroom. We recommend visiting education resource websites (we like www.educationworld.com) focused on various education topics, including copyright, and the government's copyright website (www.copyright.gov) to learn more. When in doubt, it is always beneficial to ask the author of a resource for permission, even if it might not be necessary.

KEEPING UP TO DATE WITH DIGITAL TOOLS

Keeping up to date with digital tools can seem like an insurmountable task. Admittedly, it can be challenging to stay abreast of continually emerging technology trends. However, teachers do not need to keep up with all trends; rather they should investigate the technology that is most applicable to their own classrooms and context. A first step in keeping up to date is to determine your needs and the types of technology that might be most useful for you. For example, someone who teaches reading and language arts and has a class set of iPads might be best served by trying to keep up with iPad apps that can facilitate literacy learning. This determination significantly narrows the technology that the teacher needs to keep up to date with. Therefore, we recommend first identifying your technology needs and making time to keep up with that type of tool or technology. By narrowing the type of technology for which you need to search, the task can seem less overwhelming and you become more likely to successfully achieve your goal. In addition to narrowing the type of technology for which you plan to keep up to date, we recommend four strategies, described subsequently, for remaining current on technology trends.

Develop a Professional Learning Network

One of the most certain ways to keep abreast of technology trends is to develop a Professional Learning Network (PLN) with which you interact regularly. Professional Learning Networks are a type of social network through which you use digital technology to regularly interact with colleagues, school leaders, experts, and others interested in a topic of interest to stay up to date on current trends, learn from others, and foster your professional skills. The fastest and easiest way to cultivate a PLN is through social media. Twitter is among the most commonly used tools for following trends in education. The key to using Twitter to keep up to date is to find the right people and hashtags to follow. Specifically, you want to follow people or organizations that are reputable and post information relevant to your interests. Next, you can find a list of hashtags most relevant to your interests and regularly search them. Although hashtags change and emerge frequently, there are many sites that provide current lists of hashtags relevant to education. For example, this site contains a listing of the most popular educational Twitter hashtags: http://bit.ly/1qPI1aa. Once you connect to organizations, people, and hashtags, you will find more people to follow and your network can grow. Another way to learn with Twitter is through Twitter chats. In these chats, you will follow a hashtag at a particular time and see questions posted by moderators. Anyone can respond by adding the hashtag to his or her tweet. You can simply read through the tweets or participate in the conversation by sharing your own insights or asking questions. In addition to Twitter, you can use Facebook and Pinterest to follow professional groups and bloggers related to your interests. You may also be interested in starting a school-wide PLN to connect with other teachers in your school and the resources they are using (see textbox 12.1).

Watch a Webinar

Another way to stay up to date is through webinars. Many organizations offer live and on-demand webinars for educators. When webinars are streamed live

Textbox 12.1.

Focus On:
School-Wide PLN

Challenge: Often, we find multiple teachers in a school using digital technology in meaningful and innovative ways to promote literacy. However, because of differences in grade levels taught and classroom proximity, many teachers do not communicate their ideas or resources with one another.

Consider: A digital PLN provides a method for all teachers to easily connect with one another and share resources and ideas for student learning with digital technology.

Tips:
1. Ask your instructional coach to share your Twitter or social media page with other teachers in the school, while encouraging those teachers to create their own pages. Teachers can follow one another through social media to create a PLN.
2. Aim to visit the PLN once a week to stay current on resources teachers are using in their classrooms. Someone may be planning a lesson or unit that you can use!
3. Provide positive feedback or ask questions to other teachers in the PLN to create a networked community.
4. Post links to interesting web resources and encourage other teachers to provide opinions on the PLN about ideas for using those resources.
5. If a lesson using digital technology does not go as planned, seek feedback from your PLN. Someone may have had the same experience and is able to provide insight!

Check Out: Twitter (www.twitter.com)

Although we know that Twitter may not always be the best option for student learning in K-6 grades, it does provide an excellent platform for teachers to connect with one another about professional development and using digital technology in the classroom.

to your computer you may ask questions of the presenter. Many webinars also offer a back channel so that participants can share ideas and strategies with other attendees. Webinars can also be accessed on demand, allowing teachers to watch at a time that is convenient for them.

Connect with Professional Organizations

Many professional organizations have special interest groups, online learning networks, and digital newsletters that help teachers stay up to date. For example, through www.thejournal.com, you can subscribe to numerous digital newsletters such as Common Core Tech Update, T.H.E. 21st Century School, and K12 Mobile Classroom. This site also provides a continually updated stream of K-12 educational technology news, hosts regularly scheduled webinars, and contains a bank of resources on a wide variety of educational technology topics. Other organizations that may be of interest for literacy teachers are the International Literacy Association and the National Council for Teachers of English.

Make Time to Play

One of the best ways to learn about new technologies and how to use them is to make time to experiment with them. This can be challenging and it may seem impossible to find time to do this. However, playing with digital tools does not have to take a large amount of time. This can be something that you do for as little as five minutes. Often one of the best ways you can learn more about a tool is by watching a feature video on a website. Many companies now include on their website introductory videos highlighting the features of their tool and suggesting ways to use it with students. You can also learn a lot about a tool's usefulness by quickly trying it out to see how easy it is to use. It is important to realize that you do not have to have the time to master the tool. Rather, you can benefit from simply spending a few minutes discovering the features of a tool to determine if it would be useful to learn more about.

RESOURCES FOR FINDING NEW DIGITAL TOOLS

Even when teachers stay connected and up to date with digital technology through the strategies described in the previous section, it can still be challenging to find apps. Apps may perhaps be more difficult to locate than web tools because of the ways that each of them can be searched for online. Teachers must rely more on app recommendations from websites rather than search engine results when searching for apps that may be useful in the classroom. Therefore, we wish to draw attention to two useful sites for locating apps for nearly any purpose.

First, we recommend App Crawlr (www.appcrawlr.com). App Crawlr is an app discovery engine that allows users to search for apps, choosing from a wide variety of categories, such as education, and topics, such as note taking or PDF annotation. Users can then further refine a search by specifying an audience (such as kids or teachers), features (such as Dropbox integration), or price (free or paid). The site also allows users to sort the results by relevance, by what is trending, by popularity and total number of downloads, and by lesser known apps. This site is an excellent tool for discovering apps for specific classroom purposes or for simply discovering apps that you may use in the future.

Another site that we recommend is Ed Shelf (www.edshelf.com). Ed Shelf is a site created specifically for educators. It allows users to search for apps and websites based on age, subject, platform, and category. Users can search for individual apps or collections of apps that are created by members. Each app is listed with a thorough description and provides a place for comments. With each app there is also a listing of the number of collections in which the app can be found and the number of people on the site who use the app, effectively providing a rating of the app's popularity. Apps are rated and reviewed by parents and educators. Users can also create their own collection of apps related to a particular subject, topic or use.

Although there are many sites that recommend apps, it can be overwhelming to search through them all. By narrowing a search to these two sites, or similar sites, teachers can spend less time weeding through a huge number of search results and more directly access what they need.

DEVELOPING A GAME PLAN FOR CONTINUING TO LEARN ABOUT DIGITAL TECHNOLOGY

In addition to the strategies and resources mentioned in the previous two sections, Cennamo, Ross, and Ertmer (2010) suggest that teachers can continue their learning about technology by using their GAME (Goals, Action, Monitor, Evaluate) plan technique. The first step in this technique is to identify what you need to know as specifically as possible and set that as a *goal*. The next step is to take *action* toward your goal. Ways to take action may include talking to a coach or colleague, attending a professional conference, reading books, or searching the web for information. Often, a combination of these action steps is the best approach. As you take action, the next step is to *monitor* your approach to determine if you are getting the information and resources that you need and if you need to try a different approach. Finally, you should *evaluate* your learning to determine if you have successfully met your goal, if you need to continue searching, or if you need to set a different goal. We believe that by being intentional in seeking out new information and resources, you will be more likely to remain current on new technologies and to find resources and ideas that are most relevant to your classroom.

INTEGRATING TOOLS IN SCHOOLS WITH LIMITED TECHNOLOGY RESOURCES

We recognize that even with the wide-spread use and adoption of technology in education, many schools are still limited in digital technology resources. We offer here some potential solutions for teachers who perhaps have access to only one school computer lab shared among all teachers or who only have one classroom computer for students to use. We also provide ideas for securing grant funding to purchase your own set of classroom tablets or other digital resources.

School computer labs can be tricky to navigate. Some schools only provide one, or possibly two, labs for the entire school, and often teachers must sign up for the lab weeks ahead of time. In many cases, you must simply sign up for a time that is available, and not always the most convenient for your class. Jamie, one of the authors, faced a similar situation in her first years of teaching and spent a great deal of time thinking about how to add technology-based instruction in meaningful ways into her classroom without making it an add-on whenever the computer lab was finally available. One idea that worked well was creating project-based instruction that utilized digital technology and print-based tools. That way, one lesson was never contingent on technology being available on a given date. Instead, students could complete some aspects of the project in class and some in the lab. Jamie also worked with her school media specialist so that students could use a small set of library computers in small groups during class times where students were working independently on projects.

If you only have one computer available in your classroom, you may consider creating class projects where digital technology will be used for some, but not all, of the project. Assignments for the project can be divided among small groups of students, so that the computer can be used for a portion of the project and with one group of students at a time. Or, the same can be done for small-group projects where students are working on different components of the project at different times during an activity hour, and students can rotate using the classroom computer. You can also create activity stations in your classroom to engage students in learning during a unit, with the computer serving as one of multiple learning stations that students rotate to through the stations. In this way, the computer becomes an integral part of a project or activity for all students instead of a lone machine.

For teachers with no classroom computers and very limited access to a computer lab, we also recommend preparing a grant for a class set or multiple tablets for your classroom. Some teachers may find this task less daunting if you write with another teacher, and share the set between your classes. Prominent education agencies, such as the National Education Association (NEA; visit www.nea.org/grants/grantsawardsandmore.html for more information), provide grant funds to purchase supplies, including technology, to support and improve student learning in classrooms. Teachers may also receive private funding through websites, such as Donors Choose (www.donorschoose. org), where teachers post requests for supplies and projects they would like to fund in their classroom and private donors select the projects they want to fund. Many teachers have found great success through these types of programs as you can advertise your project on Facebook or other social media to increase the number of people who see your request.

Finally, teachers may consider types of technology-focused projects and assignments they can implement in their classrooms that students can work on outside of class. We recommend surveying your students at the beginning of the school year to determine the tools they have available to them outside of class, and the proximity of public spaces, such as public libraries, that offer free computer use to your school and their homes. However, it may not always be feasible for students, particularly at the elementary level, to access these spaces outside of class. A last suggestion that we have observed teachers implement successfully is incorporating mobile technology through smart phones as an out-of-class option to use apps and access the Internet, as many parents (and students) now have access to smart phones. In this case, you would want to survey parents at the beginning of the school year to determine their willingness to allow their children to participate in mobile-based technology activities. We have found that more times than not parents are willing to provide opportunities for their children to participate in technology-based learning as these activities are often motivating and highly enriching for students and their learning.

PREPARING FOR THE BEST AND WORST

Throughout this book we have described the many ways that digital technology can support literacy instruction. You can prepare for success with digital technology by planning thoughtful instruction using the Technology Integration Planning Cycle for Literacy and Language Arts that was introduced in chapter 2. An important part of that planning cycle is considering potential barriers to integrating technology in the way you have planned. It is important to recognize that, even with careful planning, many things can go wrong when integrating technology. That is not, however, a reason for discarding technology use. Rather, we encourage you to follow a few simple guidelines to prepare for the best lesson possible, even if the worst happens.

GUIDELINE 1: TRY OUT THE TOOLS YOU ARE PLANNING TO USE

This is an important step for avoiding unexpected surprises. For example, there are websites that will allow a user to create products such as videos and presentations without an account, but do not allow the user to save them unless they sign into an account. By trying out the assignment that you wish to have students complete, you can better determine the types of problems that they may have and develop solutions for supporting them or find ways to work around the problems.

GUIDELINE 2: HAVE A BACKUP PLAN

Even with careful planning, you may still encounter problems that force you to abandon your use of technology and try something different. It is important to recognize this possibility and always have a way to continue running the classroom smoothly, even when technology fails. This will require flexibility and a willingness to try again later.

GUIDELINE 3: CREATE A CLASSROOM CULTURE FOR TECHNOLOGY USE

As with any other part of your classroom culture, it is important to create norms for technology use. For example, you will likely want to develop a standard practice for acquiring and handling digital devices, for when devices can be used, for when students should close their devices and so on. By creating this culture, the teacher does not have to continually spend instructional time providing guidelines and setting expectations.

GUIDELINE 4: CREATE TUTORIALS
AND CHEAT SHEETS

It can be frustrating to repeat the same set of directions multiple times for multiple students. However, this can easily become the norm in a digital classroom where students are experiencing new technologies on a regular basis. One way to avoid this redundancy is for the teacher to create short video tutorials and cheat sheets for digital tools that are introduced into the classroom. This way, the teacher can spend his or her time teaching the literacy curriculum and supporting students' literacy development rather than repeating instructions about how to use a particular tool.

GUIDELINE 5: DO NOT TAKE AWAY
THE DEVICE UNLESS ABSOLUTELY NECESSARY

Although there should be consequences for computer or tablet misuse, we do not believe that teachers should take away students digital devices when misuse occurs. The reason for this is that rather than being a disciplinary technique, taking away the device actually becomes a hindrance to learning. Just as a teacher would not take away pencil and paper when students become off-task, he or she should not take away the digital tool that can be used to get the student back on task.

ASSESSMENTS ALIGNED WITH
COMMON CORE STATE STANDARDS

Something that has not yet been discussed in this book, but is a relevant, timely, and important topic is standardized testing related to the Common Core State Standards. Students in most states in the United States will either take assessments created by the Partnership for Readiness of College and Careers or the Smarter Balanced Assessment Consortium to demonstrate their proficiency in areas addressed by the Common Core State Standards. These tests will be delivered through computers or tablets, and students will be expected to be familiar enough with these devices to navigate them effectively to respond to questions. At minimum, it is expected that students will need to be able to understand and respond to information delivered through video, may need to highlight or drag text on a screen, and will need to type responses they compose rather than writing them with pencil and paper. Further, students will be required to compare, contrast, and synthesize information from multiple sources. The tests will likely incorporate video clips and websites as sources of information. These changes are much different than most previous state tests and require proficiency with digital tools. The lessons suggested in this book are examples of ways that teachers can prepare students to develop the digital literacy skills that they need to read and navigate these online tests. It is important that students have such digital literacy skills so that the test results do not reflect a lack of ability to navigate and respond digitally, but rather reflects students' true academic competencies.

REFLECTION QUESTIONS

1. How will you stay up to date on digital tools? Create an action plan for remaining current on digital technologies and how you will continue to locate new and relevant resources to use in your classroom.
2. What classroom guidelines should you put into place to create a culture of appropriate technology use in your classroom?

REFERENCE

Cennamo, K., Ross, J., & Ertmer, P. (2010). *Technology integration for meaningful classroom use.* Belmont, CA: Wadsworth.

Index